THE BREAKTHROUGH MANUAL

THE
BREAKTHROUGH
MANUAL

Paul McGuire

248.8

BRIDGE PUBLISHING, INC.
South Plainfield, NJ

All Scripture has been quoted from the
New American Standard version of the Bible
unless otherwise noted.

The Breakthrough Manual
ISBN 0-88270-658-6
Library of Congress
        Catalog Card #92-74979
Copyright © 1993 by Paul McGuire

Published by:
Bridge Publishing Inc.
2500 Hamilton Blvd.
South Plainfield, NJ 07080

To my wife, Kristina, and my children,
Paul, Michael and Jennifer.

*"And I will restore to you the years
that the locust hath eaten...
And ye shall eat in plenty, and be satisfied,
and praise the name of the Lord your God,
that hath dealt wondrously with you:
and my people shall never be ashamed."*

Joel 2:25-26

Contents

ACKNOWLEDGMENTS

In writing *The Breakthrough Manual*, I received such rich inspiration from many sources. First of all, the teaching of my pastor, Jack Hayford of The Church On The Way, has made a powerful contribution to my life and ministry.

Also, I wish to thank my wonderful father and mother for having the courage to grow and demonstrate positive change. My wife Kristina has been a constant source of motivation and has challenged me to constantly press forward.

In addition, Scott Bauer, John Tolle, Dan Hicks, Keith Dawson, Chip Graves, Gary Curtis, and many others at The Church On The Way have been a constant source of encouragement, as has Ron Williams at the *Advance* and my friend Dave Otto.

Also, my thanks to Guy Morrell and the staff at Bridge Publishing Inc.

INTRODUCTION

I wrote *The Breakthrough Manual* because I have devoted a lifetime trying to discover the principles that would make my life work and in the sincere desire that after I discovered them I would be able to share these life-changing principles with others. I have literally become obsessed with the concept of breakthrough, or how a person can find the power to overcome obstacles in his or her life.

The message of this book comes directly out of the laboratory of my own life. Quite frankly, my life was a total disaster until I discovered the foundational principle of breakthrough, which is accepting Jesus Christ as my Lord and Savior. Perhaps it would be more accurate to say that I did not discover Christ at all. While it is true that I was searching, the reality of what happened is that Jesus Christ found me and let me into His kingdom.

Prior to that time I was vainly looking for answers in psychology, the New Age, destructive relationships, psychedelic drugs, and other dead-end streets. I came from a dysfunctional home environment where, even though there were some tremendously positive experiences for which I am deeply thankful, there was also the destructive force of what could be called the generational curse of alcoholism riddled throughout my family. Due to the pain and hurt of being raised in such a family, I began at an early age to search for answers to questions I had about the meaning of life.

This book is about some of the answers that I have discovered. Let me say right at the outset that this is not a book about religion or religious ideas. People who find out I have written a number of books about God, the New Age, and similar subjects invariably ask me if I am religious. This is a book about true spirituality based on biblical principles. I really dislike the word "religious." To me, being religious connotes having arguments about what kind of incense to burn or what position you should pray in. Even though I am a committed member of a local church—The Church On The Way, which I have attended for almost 13 years—I do not consider myself religious. I consider myself spiritual. In fact, it was religion that kept me from knowing Jesus Christ for many years. I saw the religion of Christianity as a barbed-wire fence keeping me from reaching out to know the person of Christ. In addition, I accepted Jesus Christ while literally fleeing from a so-called Christian religious retreat by hitchhiking on the back roads of Missouri.

To sum it all up, you could say that I am a seeker of truth and a committed Christian. Yet even after I accepted Jesus Christ, I found that many people who know

Him are living lives that are far below God's great plan for them. This book is dedicated to every person who is trying to become everything they were created to be and are simply looking for the power and resources to make it happen. *The Breakthrough Manual* is not about human engineering in order to succeed. It is about the kingdom principles Christ gave us to triumph over the adversity in our lives. *The Breakthrough Manual* is about success, but not success on the world's terms. It is about God's definition of success, which is different from man's. In short, I wrote *The Breakthrough Manual* as a tool to help those who need to break through into all that God has for them. I pray that it will be helpful sharing kingdom keys with you—the laws and principles that can transform your life for the better.

1

THE BREAKTHROUGH MANUAL

You were created to have a wonderful and rich life. Your life should not be one of drudgery, misery, and unfulfilled dreams. Your life is a gift, and it should be one of adventure and unlimited possibilities. It should be as immense and infinite as the night sky in the countryside where endless stars twinkle in celestial majesty. In the same way, your life should be overflowing with creativity and promise.

Do these words sound too lofty or unrealistic? Perhaps talk of twinkling stars and endless possibilities clashes with Monday-morning realities, unpaid bills, broken relationships, headaches, and shattered dreams. It is true there are many books on the market that promise you power and the keys to success. Yet the common theme of all such books is that you can get what you want in life if you try harder and develop the mental skills to succeed.

This book contains powerful keys that will enable you to become an overcomer in life and triumph in the midst of adversity. However, the keys to success offered throughout this book are not dependent upon your mental skills or your physical strength. It is true you will have to be available to participate, cooperate, and even obey. But the power to help you win will not come from yourself, but from a power above and beyond yourself. In the final analysis, it is the Creator's power that can bring your life together. Every single book and success system known to man is contingent upon the will, energy, and discipline of the follower to see him or her through. The problem is that life, sooner or later, will throw up obstacles that are too great for a person to overcome. It is at these times that the truly wise person understands that he or she needs help from above and that help from above is divine and not human. Any system of thought or practice which removes God from the equation is sadly lacking. It is God alone who can give us the power we need to triumph over life's adversities.

THE GARDEN OF EDEN REVISITED

Many people in our culture believe that the historical account of Adam and Eve in the Garden of Eden is a fairy tale and should not be taken seriously. They believe instead that man accidently came into being through the random process of evolution, even though modern statisticians tell us through computer research that the odds of that really happening would be equivalent to an explosion in a printing plant creating an English dictionary. The point is that the account of a real Adam and Eve being created by a real, infinite God has a lot more credibility than the primordial soup theory we call evolution.

What really matters is that if you went back to the beginning of time and visited Adam and Eve, you would see the kind of world God intended for the human race. It was there in the Garden of Eden that the Lord built a perfect world for men and women. It was a beautiful place with trees, waterfalls, flowers. Adam and Eve had everything a couple could want.

If you contrast Adam and Eve's world with ours, you can see that we have not progressed with civilization but regressed. Here on planet Earth, centuries later, we have pollution, serial killers, traffic jams, sickness, poverty, divorce, drugs, and suicide. Like the cigarette commercial goes, "You've come a long way, baby!" Backwards!

The Garden of Eden was a real place where a real Adam and Eve lived. All of contemporary society originates out of the fall of man in the Garden of Eden. Basically, what is meant by the term "the fall of man" is that Adam and Eve deliberately chose to step out of Paradise by deliberately disobeying God who warned them that if they ate from a certain tree they would die. In short, when Adam and Eve disobeyed God, the life force or divine energy that kept them alive eternally and powered Eden was short-circuited.

THE FALL OF MAN

It is impossible to understand or correct any problem in life without first understanding the root of the problem. Fundamentally, we must understand that all of life's problems have a primary source and that is what the Bible calls *sin*. Sin is a very real, cosmic force responsible for the destruction and death of both people and society.

When we go back to the Garden of Eden, we see that the personal, living God of the universe created man in His own image.

> Then God said, "Let Us make man in Our image, according to Our likeness; and let them rule over the fish of the sea and over the birds of the sky and over the cattle and over all the earth, and over every creeping thing that creeps on the earth." And God created man in His own image, in the image of God He created him; male and female He created them (Gen. 1:26-27 NAS).

Here we see a number of fundamental, basic principles about man and the universe:

1. Each man and woman alive is created in the image of the real God.
2. All human beings were created to rule over life and their environment. People were not created to be victims of life or any circumstance.
3. Each man and woman alive can have a powerful self-image and identity because they are created in God's image. All people have value and worth because they are created in the image of God.

Here we see primary principles about life and man's existence. First, there is *The Principle of Identity* which states that men and women can know who they really are because they are the children of an infinite God. This principle directly clashes with modern thought which teaches that man is the accidental product of random chemical mixtures, or evolution. Existentialism and evolution are mythological belief systems which strip the human race of its divine origins. These faulty philosophical systems of thought are directly responsible for the loss of meaning in contemporary culture. These belief systems inevitably produce many evils, because once you teach man that his life is meaningless, then his actionso (good or bad) have no meaning.

The net result of this is moral anarchy which produces child abuse, murder, theft, mass killings, a consumer culture, and pervasive despair. It is no accident that here in America we have an unprecedented suicide rate among teenagers. As a nation, we have literally become bankrupt in terms of vision and purpose. Even American Indian cultures and other tribal nations imparted a basic belief system which incorporated meaning and purpose to its offspring. Only recently in Western cultures have entire generations been raised in a spiritual vacuum.

The second principle that can be found here is *The Principle of Dominion,* which teaches us that men and women were not created or made by the Great Designer to be victims of life's circumstances or environment. Essentially, this means that man was supposed to be in control of food, clothing, shelter, and other life support systems. However, it also means that man was not supposed to be a slave to false ideological systems, human governments, corporations, technologies, and the like. In short, man was not created to be a slave to his environment or to other men. Yet, we see the majority of people on planet Earth in various forms of cultural and economic slavery.

Both *The Principle of Identity* and *The Principle of Dominion* are true principles in the created universe. In essence, they are true because they represent true truth or final reality. They are not based on man-made myth but on the way the universe really works. Christianity is truth. Man has worth and dignity because he or she is a created being made in the image of God. This understanding always produces revolutionary freedom in a society. Truth is the antidote for slavery and totalitarianism, both of which strip man of his true meaning and purpose and paves the way for manipulation, brainwashing, and totalitarian control.

Real personal breakthrough must have a philosophical base and that base is who we really are as children of a real God. This truth cannot be tampered with. It is basic to the survival of the individual, the family, and civilization. In our time there has been a conspiracy against this truth. The purpose of *The Breakthrough Manual* is to reignite our understanding of this fundamental truth so that the reader can be empowered and released to be all he or she was created to be. Yet, in order for the "breakthrough" to happen, there must first be a proper understanding of the truth of identity and purpose.

2

PSYCHOLOGICAL MANIFESTATIONS
OF THE FALL

In the Garden of Eden, God specifically warned Adam and Eve not to eat from the tree of the knowledge of good and evil.

> And the Lord God commanded the man, saying, "From any tree of the garden you may eat freely; but from the tree of the knowledge of good and evil you shall not eat, for in the day that you eat from it you shall surely die" (Gen. 2:16-17).

Here in the middle of the Garden, God basically said, "Take care of the Garden and otherwise do whatever you want; just don't eat of the tree of the knowledge of good and evil." The modern equivalent would be a parent saying to a toddler as it is put in a wonderful room full of toys, "Have fun in the room and play with all the toys; just don't touch the electrical socket."

Here are Adam and Eve enjoying their habitation and having an incredible time. God is saying, "Enjoy yourselves." Then He warns them about this tree only because it has the capacity to destroy them. God was not withholding anything good from Adam and Eve. He was holding back evil knowledge and negative energy.

However, another element is added to this scenario, and that is the reality of "personal evil in the universe," or Satan. In addition to the issue of Adam and Eve's obedience, there is a whole other dimension to the issue and that is *a very real war between good and evil in the invisible realm*. The serpent who is at war with God is maneuvering to gain control of planet Earth and the human race by tempting Adam and Eve to eat the forbidden fruit. The reason he is doing this is because he knows that if he can get them to do this, it will remove them from God's protection

Sin should be thought of in real terms. It is a powerful, negative, and destructive force that brings death, sickness, ignorance, loss of power, confusion, and other real problems. Sin is a dark force which promises liberation but instead actually robs people of power. It is important to understand this. When we say people are sinners, we are actually saying more than they are being bad or naughty. We are also saying that being sinners deprives people of access to God's power. In addition, one of the primary manifestations of sin is a loss of understanding that one is *in* sin. In other words, the sinner is blinded to his predicament by the very fact that he *is* a sinner.

How else can you explain this amazing situation? Physical death is an undeniable fact. You and I are dying in our physical bodies right now even as we speak. The physical universe is deteriorating and winding down. Physicists call this *The Law of Entropy*. Yet only a fool would think that it is right and natural for us to die. The fact that we exist and that our bodies are decomposing even as we speak is not the way things are supposed to be! People were never created to die and disintegrate. This is absolutely horrible beyond words! Yet in our culture there is a kind of mass, collective denial of this fact. This is why people sob and weep at funerals. It is a primal acknowledgment that this is wrong, and it is! Death is wrong. Death is unnatural. It has only become natural because we are in a fallen world infected with a cosmic death force called sin.

What happened in the Garden of Eden is that man forgot who he was. With the fall of man came a loss of memory and understanding of who we really are. This loss of understanding and memory has now become part of our culture and our society. We are not mere people or evolved animals. You and I are the very children of a real, infinite God. We have purpose and identity. We are here for a reason, and there is a way back home to God. God, in His endless, Fatherly love for the human race, sent a means by which we could come back to God and live with Him forever. Jesus Christ, the Savior of mankind, came and died on a cross and was resurrected so that the power of sin could be broken and the enormous power of eternal life could infuse us with living energy so powerful that it would resurrect us from the dead.

Imagine the force of Niagara Falls, or lightning, or the immense power which causes the sun to rise and the day to dawn; the force behind the flowers of spring, the birth of a child, or the countless stars glistening in the night sky. It is the power of the living God that is responsible for these phenomena. That power is still available to us today.

Since the fall of man produced a loss of understanding, it follows that accepting Christ by faith can produce a renewal of the human mind. Although human beings are much more than machines, the process could be remotely likened to a computer that's been turned off and gathering dust which is cleaned, turned on, and booted up. It is amazing what the computer can do when it is turned on—a whole world of possibilities exists.

The problem impairing the saving knowledge of Jesus Christ is that the power of the message and the original meaning have been distorted through the years. It is true that there have been great men and women of God who understood the power of the Gospel of Jesus Christ, such as the Apostle Paul, Martin Luther, Charles Finney, and many others. In addition, there have been revivals and great movements of God. Yet despite these movements, the power of the original message of the Gospel of Jesus Christ has been diluted and distorted in many areas of our culture. In teaching the saving power of the Gospel of Jesus Christ, it is necessary to speak to the culture of our day, in a language that it will understand, the truth of Christ's message. This entails acting as modern linguists and communicating God's truth in contemporary terms in the same way missionaries study native languages and communicate the Bible in a way that those whom they minister to can understand.

However, here in the Western societies we have not adequately done this and thus we are seeing the wholesale destruction of our culture. Certainly, we *say* we have "preached the Gospel," but we have most certainly not. Instead, we have diluted and distorted it. When the power of the Gospel is communicated properly, it always brings total and radical change.

When truth is presented understandably, it inevitably creates revolutionary change and transformation. This should not imply that the Gospel creates anything weird, or frightening. The Gospel produces crystal-clear sanity and reason. It is rational, but not confined to contemporary rationalizations that reduce its power or impact into cultural norms. It must be understood that the communication of the true Gospel of Jesus Christ always produces revolutionary change in both the individual and the culture.

The message of the Gospel entails the total transformation of the human personality. Not in a limited psychological sense, but like a chrysalis which becomes a butterfly, it is a total transformation of the human being from mortal to divine. We are not talking about inner healing or therapy. We are talking about "Lazarus, come forth!" You don't put Lazarus in a counseling center wrapped in his burial cloths. You stand in the power and authority of Jesus Christ and command him to come forth! As such, the power of the Gospel can only be understood when we speak with the authority of a personal God and experience the infusion of life force and a mighty baptism of the Holy Spirit of the infinite, personal, living God of the universe.

3

THE BROKEN DREAM

Adam was the original Dad and Eve the original Mom of the whole human race. Yet when they fell from grace in the Garden of Eden, a fatal flaw entered the family unit: sin. Every family since then has been affected by the fall.

It was God's original plan to make the family a place of total love and acceptance that could build strong and whole people. But people everywhere are emotionally wounded by broken families. Now all of us have to live with a distorted image of marriage and the family. I understand those fears because I come from a troubled home where the marriage did not work. As a result, for many years I believed that marriage was obsolete and unnecessary.

For many people marriage has become a broken dream. But the Creator of the universe has a way of restoring broken dreams and, through the healing in my own marriage, I was able to see the love and power that can be released when a husband and wife learn to live in the fullness of God's blessing for their lives. The marriage relationship becomes a source of power and healing for individuals. Families become a true home for the weary and the tired. If you have a real home to go to, you have a real, God-given refuge.

Adam and Eve had a good thing going as they fell in love in the Garden of Eden. But Christ has made provisions for men and women to experience a taste of heaven in their own homes. Families can be the most powerful source of blessing in our lives if we will let the Creator recreate them in His original design.

THE ORIGINAL FAMILY

The family has been called the building block of civilization and it is certainly true that each individual's self-image, mind set, behavior patterns, and ability to relate are established in the childhood years. But these days we hear a lot of talk regarding dysfunctional families. A recent guest expert on a national television talk show stated the belief that, "Ninety percent of America's families are dysfunctional."

According to the Bible, the first parents of the entire human race were Adam and Eve, who established the first monogamous male and female relationship as well as the first family. Yet there were some remarkable differences between Adam and Eve and contemporary marriages and families.

First of all, Adam and Eve were created directly in the image of God. Genesis 1:26 reads: "Then God said, 'Let

Us make man in Our image, according to Our like-
ness....'" And then it states in verse 27, "And God created man in His own image, in the image of God He
created him; male and female He created them." Here
we see that man and woman were both made in the image of God.

In addition, they were created in a state of perfect harmony and oneness with God. Prior to the fall, they lived
in a completely different state of consciousness than the
human race does now. Their minds and bodies were
completely filled with the light of God and they were in
a state of oneness with Him. They lived in a perfect state
of peace and total love.

Also, they lived in the innocent state of little children.
Adam and Eve were naked but were not ashamed.

Thus, the first family of Adam and Eve was a perfect
family with a perfect marriage. This perfect psychological state of being produced a couple who had a perfect
self-image: no fears or insecurities, no neuroses, no vic-
timization patterns, and nothing of the sort. Adam and
Eve lived in complete psychological and spiritual wholeness prior to the fall. Adam and Eve were extremely
powerful, creative, joyous, energetic, loving, secure, and
positive people because they were made directly in God's
image. Their minds did not have to be renewed, because
they were already perfect.

Today, many generations after the fall of man, sin continues to affect the lives of every man and woman on
planet Earth. The result is that people today are prey to
such dysfunctions as low self-esteem, loss of identity, sexual confusion, fear, poor self-image, addictive behaviors,

powerlessness, mental health problems, and an entire host of psychological and spiritual disorders. Yet the prime root of these disorders is the fall of man and sin.

SALVATION: THE SOLUTION TO ALL PROBLEMS

The Bible states that the cure for all your problems lies in a term called salvation. Yet this concept of salvation has lost its meaning to the culture at large today. Salvation should mean the complete and total rescuing, healing, and empowering of your life after you accept Jesus Christ as Lord of your life. Salvation is about a real and powerful, personal living God of the universe breaking through the darkness, coming into your life on a personal level, and setting you free. When people accept Jesus Christ by faith into their lives and experience salvation, they are saved from their sins and instantly made right with God.

However, their minds must still be renewed or reprogrammed in order that they might begin to function at their optimum level. This renewing or reprogramming of the mind is part of God's plan of redemption for the human race: to be saved in your soul and to be ready for eternity. Living with a mind that is filled with darkness, confusion, loss of identity, purposelessness, powerlessness, poor self-image, dysfunction, and addictive behaviors was never God's plan for the human race. The Gospel of Jesus Christ speaks to your life now in nitty-gritty details and promises you a new mind set which will empower you to live successfully as a person of purpose and power in the midst of a fallen world.

Accepting Jesus Christ as your Lord and Savior is the most powerful first step of freedom you can take. But you must continue to walk the path of renewing your mind so that you can grow into the powerful person God wants you to be!

4

THE LONG AND WINDING ROAD
TO GET BACK HOME

Paul McCartney, the former Beatle, sings that classic song with the lyrics about "the long and winding road to get back homeward." This expresses all of our deepest desires to find a real home for our lives. The expulsion of Adam and Eve from the Garden of Eden has had very real consequences in our lives today. The pollution of our cities, crowded streets, stock market crashes, the war in the Middle East, and other problems all have as their root the fall of man. In fact, all of man's inner problems such as insecurity, loneliness, depression, and a poor self-image, are all psychological manifestations of the fall.

You and I were created for something greater then a second-hand world. Look at little children when you take them to the beach. They laugh with delight and run down the beach giggling as the waves splash their feet. Jesus said, "Unless you become like little children, you shall never enter the kingdom of heaven." Children know how to play and have a sense of fun and joy in life. This is the way God created you and me to live, with laughter and delight. In order to experience breakthrough and be saved through faith in Christ, we are going to have to regain that simple, childlike faith and trust in God.

The Bible teaches us that the only way to get back home and enter the kingdom of heaven is to have the faith and trust of a little child. That means forgetting the cynical reality that adulthood brings and once again being really open to God's goodness.

I remember, when I first was presented with the message of the Gospel of Jesus Christ, how terrified I was to really open up my soul and invite Christ in. The person who shared his faith with me compared it to a little child standing on a fence and jumping into his father's arms. The father would catch and lovingly embrace the child as he or she jumped. However, I had trouble with that imagery, because I had a stronghold in my mind about real trust which related to an incident in my childhood when I was at the beach with my father.

My Dad carried me into the surf on his shoulders and I was trusting in him. Suddenly a big wave came and knocked him down and swept me off his shoulders under the water. For a moment, as a little child, I felt as if I was drowning and I was terrified. Although my father could not help it, this force of the wave created a sense of distrust in me, and for quite a while afterwards I was unable to enjoy playing in the ocean. So, when I was told that I needed to open up to God and jump off the fence emotionally and intellectually into the arms of a loving God, I was afraid to do it. Then one day, while hitchhiking on the back roads of Missouri, I invited Christ into my life. Then, when I leapt off the fence into the arms of a loving, heavenly Father who caught me and embraced me with His love, I discovered that I could trust Him completely.

5

EARTH SCHOOL

I believe that today many, many people have wrong and destructive ideas of what real Christianity is all about. They may concentrate on such "outward observances" as weekly church attendance, charitable giving, and attempting to live a moral life. All of these are important, but there is something more. Everyone should know that true biblical Christianity is about discovering the reality of God in life. It is a life-transforming experience.

We live in a fallen world where many things tend toward decay and destruction. This does not mean, however, that we shouldn't become involved and attempt to make positive changes. But, it does mean that we are to understand the fact that this present world is not our home. We are in what could be called *Earth School*. The purpose of *Earth School* is to educate us and prepare us to live forever in a place called eternity. God is using the present circumstances and challenges to teach us how to rule and reign with Him forever.

It is important to understand that the reason God gave us guidelines for living was to keep us free. God requires of His people basic spiritual and moral disciplines to protect them. But the emphasis of true biblical Christianity should be on what God is preparing us for.

As children of God, we are destined to live in another world—in eternity—where we are going to have incredible things to do. Heaven is going to be a world of unlimited exploration and discovery. Heaven is going to be the place where you find total fulfillment as a person. Most importantly, your destiny as a Christian is to live with God forever.

The other big mistake people make while in *Earth School* is to regard the things of this present life as entirely unimportant. It is important to remember that God gave life to each of us for a purpose. Family, friends, sex, money, dreams, careers, homes, and the like are all important. You are here for a reason and not just to drift through life like a cloud. The point is that you should always view this life through an eternal perspective. You have an identity beyond this present life.

God has given you this life as a gift while you are in *Earth School.* But you are not to live this life as merely natural men and women. In other words, people who do not know God get all hung up in money, careers, relationships, homes, and such, because for them that's all there is.

But you and I have found God and have tasted heaven. We are not just running around in the darkness, for we have seen the light. *Earth School* can be an incredible adventure. But, just remember, this world is not our home. We have a real home in heaven on the other side of life. This home is more real than the chair you are sitting in, and God has a place for you there. One of the lessons of *Earth School* is that we are just traveling through this lifetime on the way to forever.

6

THE MANUFACTURER'S HANDBOOK ON LIFE

Don't you wish that when you were young someone had given you a book entitled "How to Live Life"? Well, the truth is that such a book exists. In fact, this book could accurately be called *The Manufacturer's Handbook on Life*. The Great Designer of life —God —gave us His "Manufacturers Handbook on Life" called the Bible. Though the Bible was written by many people over many centuries, it was completely inspired by God and is today the Christian's sole authoritative source for knowledge of how we, as Christians, are to believe and how we are to act while we are on planet Earth. The Bible is intensely practical. In order to live life at its fullest, we need to read the Bible in practical terms.

Martin Luther translated the Bible into German because he knew how important it was for Christians to have the Bible in their own language so they could read it for themselves. Many reformation churches still have the Bible placed in front of the pulpit or altar facing towards the congregation symbolizing that the ordinary person can go directly to God and His Word.

It is important to understand Christianity in terms of presenting reality to the lost. Christ's message is real. The Bible is *The Manufacturer's Handbook on Living*. God is a Person we can know intimately, now, at this moment. The message of the Bible is that God is really alive now and it contains the history of God's relationship to men and women.

There is life-changing power in that fact. What counts is the fact that God is really alive and is very much involved in people's lives. This is what the Bible is about. That is how the truth of the Bible should be communicated today.

7

HOW FEAR CAME INTO THE HUMAN RACE

One of the first things that happened after Adam and Eve disobeyed God in the Garden of Eden is that fear came into the human race. Genesis 3:9-10 reads, "Then the Lord God called to the man, and said to him, 'Where are you?' And he said, 'I heard the sound of Thee in the garden, and I was afraid because I was naked; so I hid myself.'" We see two things here. To begin with we see that, for the first time, fear was introduced into the human mind. Prior to this event, Adam and Eve knew nothing of fear. Second, we see the introduction of what modern therapists and psychologists have been talking about for years. That is the shame-based and guilt-based feelings people have. Yet both fear and shame did not exist before the fall.

This incident reveals one of the most cataclysmic events ever to have happened to mankind and that is the beginning of a fear-based, rather than a faith-based, human consciousness. Ever since the fall, mankind has been plagued by a fear-based consciousness. Fear became an integral part of man's existence.

After the fall, man began to live with a consciousness of fear rather than faith. It became natural to think in terms of failure, limitation, and lack, rather than boldly going forth and making dreams come true. The fall produced a mind set both self-limiting and self-defeating. It is now natural to be afraid of being all that we are created to be.

Psychologists talk a lot about comfort zones in the human mind. Behavioral scientists teach that the human mind naturally seeks a place of equilibrium. Many people, even though they are troubled and unhappy, nonetheless make little or no effort to help themselves because they are afraid of the unknown. According to these scientists, if people are used to poverty, abuse, addiction, and other self-limiting behaviors, they will subconsciously seek to avoid growing beyond their comfort zones because this will involve venturing into unknown territory.

The unrenewed mind seeks comfort zones, even if they are self-destructive, in order to keep an equilibrium. In order to experience breakthrough, however, we must move from fear to faith. We must renew our minds and develop a consciousness of faith and believing.

In Matthew 14:22-31 we see a perfect illustration of a faith-based mind encountering a fear-based mind:

> And immediately He made the disciples get into the boat, and go ahead of Him to the other side,

while He sent the multitudes away. And after He had sent the multitudes away, He went up to the mountain by Himself to pray; and when it was evening, He was there alone. But the boat was already many stadia away from the land, battered by the waves; for the wind was contrary. And in the fourth watch of the night He came to them, walking upon the sea. And when the disciples saw Him walking on the sea, they were frightened, saying, "It's a ghost!" And they cried out for fear. But immediately Jesus spoke to them, saying, "Take courage, it is I; do not be afraid." And Peter answered Him and said, "Lord, if it is You, command me to come to you on the water." And He said, "Come!" And Peter got out of the boat, and walked on the water and came toward Jesus. But seeing the wind, he became afraid, and beginning to sink, he cried out, saying, "Lord, save me!" And immediately Jesus stretched out His hand and took hold of him and said to him, "O you of little faith, why did you doubt?"

I believe that one purpose of this account is to teach us principles to renew our minds and to think like people of power and faith. First, we see that Jesus Christ had to separate himself and the disciples from the multitudes. Walking on water is reserved for the true disciples of Christ. Second, even Jesus Christ had to get away and pray before the power could be released for Him to walk on the water.

Third, we see the disciples were afraid when they saw Jesus Christ walking on the water. Can you imagine being in the boat with the winds blowing, with the water rocking the boat, and all of a sudden you see Jesus walking upon the waves? But while He was walking on the water, He told them not to be afraid. They were viewing the situation from their fallen, fear-based minds. Their fallen minds had a great deal of difficulty believing that all things are possible with God. Jesus Christ was trying to renew their minds and help them reach a place where they could learn to think again and believe in the power of God.

Peter had the fortitude to attempt to grasp the lesson Christ was teaching and, for a few moments, he began to walk on the water. But when he began to take his eyes off God, he became afraid and fell back into the water.

Jesus Christ admonished Peter and told him not be afraid! The Lord was trying to teach Peter and the rest of us that we must move from our old fear-based, fallen minds to a faith-based consciousness which truly believes in God's unlimited power. The reason so many individual Christians and the Church are so often powerless and defeated is that they have not learned to do this. They are still living in defeat because they have fallen minds that need to be renewed. God wants us to renew our minds and learn how to think like children of God.

God wants us to live life from the place of a renewed mind. One of the primary characteristics of a renewed mind is that we live in faith—not fear. We keep our eyes focused on God and His unlimited resources, not our inadequacies. The problems of life are not supposed to keep you down. God's supernatural resources are available to enable us to overcome our problems. We need to renew our minds and learn how to think in terms of possibilities, miracles, breakthroughs, answers, wisdom, healing, grace, and divine strength. We are not supposed to be living as merely natural men and women. We are supposed to be people of destiny, power, and purpose. God is on our side and He wants to send His power to help us.

GOD'S POWER FOR YOU IN THE NOW OF LIFE

We are not talking about unreality or escapism, but about intense practicality and purpose. God does not want His children bound by fear and by natural circumstances. The biblical accounts of the lives of faithful men and women who believed God were designed to renew your minds so that you could break free from the cycles of addiction and despair, so that you could be healed and delivered from those things that would keep you from victory. These real life accounts were written so that you could overcome and triumph in the middle of intense problems! The power of the Gospel of Jesus Christ is about your life right now, in whatever situation you are in. God has an answer for you! God has power, resources and solutions for you. You are not trapped! The situation is not hopeless! Your life is not over and you don't have to settle for a life of mediocrity and pain. You don't have to be exploited and abused. You don't have to be a victim in life anymore.

Jesus Christ said, "You shall know the truth and the truth shall set you free!" There is real power behind those words. They release kingdom energy. It means you can be set free from addiction to anything , that depression and fear cannot withstand the force of those words. It means that sickness flees from the power of God's presence, that the strength of God can come upon you. Like David, you can overcome your Goliath. We are talking about God's reality, which is the only real reality, and the power of His kingdom. We are talking about the kingdom of God overthrowing the kingdom of darkness in your life and the life of your loved ones and setting you free forever! We are talking about a total revolution in the life you are now living. Yes, there is a power so great that it defies your imagination and that power is nothing less than the power of a real God who is good and who cares.

8

UNDERSTANDING
THE SLAVE MENTALITY

After the fall of man, a specific type of mentality began to be introduced into the human race. This attitude or mind set is what Rev. Jack Hayford, senior pastor of The Church On The Way, has termed *The Slave Mentality.* Originally, when Adam and Eve walked with God in Paradise, mankind was free. However, after the fall, men and women became slaves to sin and under the dominion of the devil. It was Satan who tempted Adam and Eve to disobey God by falsely promising them deity. What really happened is that Adam and Eve went from being people of dominion and rulership to becoming slaves of sin.

We read, in Genesis 3:17-19, of the curse of sin that was placed on Adam.

> Cursed is the ground because of you; in toil you
> shall eat of it all the days of your life. Both thorns

and thistles it shall grow for you; and you shall eat the plants of the field; by the sweat of your face you shall eat bread, till you return to the ground, because from it you were taken; for you are dust, and to dust you shall return.

We see that Adam, who once had dominion of his world, is now a slave.

The Slave Mentality is a belief system in which the individual views him- or herself as someone who is under the control of another person or system. They perceive themselves as powerless people and victims. The slave is someone who must bitterly endure mistreatment and oppression in a system in which all his or her dreams are cruelly crushed.

The Slave Mentality is imbedded deep within the consciousness of modern man. Many of the things which people do today are simply reactions against the slave mentality. The fear of poverty is an example. How often do we hear stories of people who become incredibly successful, and yet act as if they are poor by clinging to every possession they have and being absurdly frugal? Where do you think such attitudes come from? They come from the fear of being poor again.

Why do you think people will do anything to be rich, to gain prestige, to be one of the elite? Because they still have the slave mentality, and they are hoping these external things will set them free.

Another characteristic of the slave mentality is, even after slaves are set free, they often still think, act, and talk like slaves. People who have been poor and have lived like slaves and then suddenly become wealthy, often lavishly indulge themselves with high-priced clothes, cars, and homes. This conspicuous spending is a reaction to their former condition.

After the fall, the entire human race was in a condition of slavery. However, Jesus Christ came to set the captives free. People who have accepted Christ are no longer slaves.

Even though they are free, however, they may still manifest the slave mentality. This present world system is a slave system where the god of this age rules people through deception and false promises. The message of the world system is that you must look out for yourself, no matter what, in order to get what you want.

Satan is the god of this world and, because of this, many people who do evil prosper for a time. But Jesus Christ has set the captives free and is in the process of setting up a new heaven and a new earth based on love and righteousness. The revolution goes on here by those who believe in God.

SETTING THE SLAVES FREE

In the book of Exodus, we read the account of how God's people, the Israelites, were forced to become slaves of Pharaoh. Basically this story typifies how God's people were slaves to the world system under Satan and how God delivers His people. In Exodus, we read how the taskmasters forced the Hebrew slaves to make bricks out of straw. However, the taskmasters were angry at the children of Israel because Moses had been raised as a deliverer of the people. So, to punish the Hebrew slaves, their straw was taken away; yet the taskmasters demanded that just as many bricks be made, even though there was no straw to make them with. It was a cruel trick to play on the Israelites.

Even though the Egyptian taskmasters forced them into hard labor, the Israelites had learned to accept their lot as slaves. When Moses came along to deliver them, he rocked the boat. The Hebrew slaves had no faith in God and did not look forward to their deliverance from bondage. Instead of hating the Egyptians and trusting God to deliver them through Moses, they became angry at their leader. They said to Moses, "May the Lord look upon you and judge you, for you have made us odious in Pharaoh's sight and in the sight of his servants, to put a sword in their hand to kill us" (Exod. 5:21).

The Israelites had completely forgotten about God's promise to deliver them out of the Pharaoh's hands. They had developed *The Slave Mentality* and were think-ing like victims instead of people who had a covenant with the living God. He had promised to bless them if they showed faith in Him. One of the characteristics of slaves, or people who have been captured by terrorists or kidnappers, is that they may begin to identify with their oppressors. This is an aspect of *The Slave Mentality*. The Israelites had stopped seeing themselves as the peo-ple of God, but rather as slaves to Pharaoh. They had lost their true identity as a people who had regained do-minion and rulership through God's covenant

In Isaiah 61:1-7, the Prophet Isaiah reads the same words that the Savior Jesus Christ repeated, which are a declaration of freedom to those with a slave mentality.

What these words are saying is that God has set you free and you must begin to think of yourself as other than a slave. We Christians are the sons and daughters of God, and we have a rich inheritance. Remember, a slave has no inheritance, but a child of the King of the universe has an enormous one. The key is to think not as a slave of the world system, but as you really are in Christ, which is an inheritor of God's kingdom.

> The Spirit of the Lord God is upon me,
> Because the Lord has anointed me,
> To bring good news to the afflicted;
> He has sent me to bind up the
>   brokenhearted,
> To proclaim liberty to captives,
> And freedom to the prisoners;
> To proclaim the favorable year of the Lord,
> And the day of vengeance of our God;
> To comfort all who mourn,
> To grant those who mourn in Zion,
> Giving them a garland instead of ashes,
> The oil of gladness instead of mourning,
> The mantle of praise instead of a spirit
>   of fainting.
> So they will be called the oaks of
>   righteousness,
> The planting of the Lord, that He may be
>   glorified.
> Then they will rebuild the ancient ruins,
> They will raise up the former devastations,
> And they will repair the ruined cities,

The desolations of many generations.
And strangers will stand and pasture your flocks,
And foreigners will be your farmers and your
   vinedressers.
But you will be called the priests of the Lord;
You will be spoken of as ministers of our God.
You will eat the wealth of nations,
And in their riches you will boast.
Instead of your shame you will have a double
   portion,
And instead of humiliation they will shout for joy
   over their portion.
Therefore they will possess a double portion in
   their land,
Everlasting joy will be theirs.

Here we see a declaration of freedom from the slave mentality! Here we see God giving us a new identity, not as slaves, but as people who will "eat the wealth of nations," who will "possess a double portion." That is what God promises for us.

9

HOW YOU CAN BREAK FREE FROM THE SLAVE MENTALITY

The key principle to be learned here is that *you are not who other people say you are, you are not who the world says you are, and you are not who you think you are unless your thoughts are in line with the Word of God. You are who God says you are in His Word.*

We are barraged daily with messages from the environment all around us about who we are. In our culture, people get their identity from their looks, their bank accounts, their zip codes, the type of car they own, their accomplishments, and their children. But all of these things do not determine who we really are. In reality, we are all only one thing, and that is *who God says we are.*

First, we cannot let outside circumstances determine our identity. Because of his great love for his son, Joseph's father gave him a coat of many colors. In addition, God sent Joseph a dream concerning his fortunate future. Joseph then made the mistake of bragging about this dream to his brothers. Being extremely jealous of Joseph, his brothers then sold him into slavery.

Joseph had a difficult path to God's calling. Yet, God was with him all through his slavery. Joseph did not allow his identity to be formed by his slavery, but by who he was in God.

When the wife of Potiphar enticed Joseph, he refused. Joseph stayed pure before the Lord; therefore, the Lord gave him prophetic dreams which would eventually usher him into royalty and rulership. Joseph did not succumb to the slave mentality. Instead, he drew his identity from the Lord and acted accordingly.

You and I have been given a coat of many colors from our heavenly Father if we could but see it in the invisible realm. God has given each one of us a fabulous destiny, no matter what our earthly station in life. The reality of God's blessing upon our life is certain and definite. We need to learn how to see it through the eyes of faith.

Another person who did not allow his identity to be formed by what others thought and said of him, and who learned how to break the slave mentality, was David. At the beginning, when David went down to meet the giant Goliath, his brothers were, to put it mildly, not happy to see him. First Samuel 17:28 tells us:

> Eliab his oldest brother heard when he spoke to his men; and Eliab's anger burned against David and he said, "Why have you come down? And with whom have you left those few sheep

in the wilderness? I know your insolence and the wickedness in your heart; for you have come down in order to see the battle."

David was basically being told, "Go back and tend the sheep, because you are too immature to be part of a man's world." But David was God's anointed one, and it was he who would slay the giant. If David had listened to his brother, he would have gone home. Instead, David got his identity and purpose from God.

We cannot allow friends, family, or society to try to tell us who we are. We must get our identity from God's Word. There are many powerful things God wants to do in each of our lives. But first we must think the way God wants us to think in order to fulfill the purpose He has for us. We cannot continue to think as slaves and fulfill God's calling for our lives if we are going to minister to others and participate in the great task of world evangelization.

We must first come into our inheritance by renewing our minds. God has created us as powerful people with the potential to change our world for the better.

We must gain the knowledge of who we really are in Christ. Fantastic opportunities await us! Doors of enormous potential will open for us and callings beyond our wildest dreams. In Jesus Christ, we are people of power and purpose. God wants to use each one of us to help others and to change our world

We must renew our minds to the fact that we are people of wisdom and power. In fact, we are royalty and a special people who have been given unique gifts and talents. This is the ultimate reality about our lives.

The Gospel is not just about eternity. It is also about who you are right now. We must know the liberating truth of who God says we are. It must become an antidote for despair and disillusionment.

The personal, living God of the universe wants to infuse your personality with the power and wonder of the message of redemption. You are no longer just John or Suzie Smith from Main Street, USA. You are now in Christ and you have a completely new identity. You are literally in the family of the God of the universe. The effect of that truth in your mind and being should have the net effect of totally transforming you and empowering you. Literally, it should foster a dynamic creativity in your personality. You have been released to be everything you were created to be. You have a dream inside you just like Joseph and you are wearing a many-colored robe in the invisible realm.

The next step is for you to *act like who you really are!* Grow strong in Christ and move in the power of blessing. You are just like Joseph, David, Daniel, Mary, and all the other heroes and heroines in the Bible. God wants you to become strong in the grace of His Son so that you can be an instrument of blessing and purpose on this dark planet. The time has come for you to begin to be who you really are. God has placed a dream inside of you. Listen to it and follow it!

10

STRONGHOLDS IN YOUR MIND

The Bible talks about strongholds existing in our minds. The Apostle Paul said:

> For though we walk in the flesh, we do not war according to the flesh, for the weapons of our warfare are not of the flesh, but divinely powerful for the destruction of fortresses (strongholds). We are destroying speculations and every lofty thing raised up against the knowledge of God, and we are taking every thought captive to the obedience of Christ (2 Cor. 10: 3-5).

The Rev. Jack Hayford defines strongholds as high things and thoughts in our minds—things that rise up to cast a shadow in our minds and thoughts, devices to injure us. Pastor Hayford talks about strongholds as "satanic debates against us, such as discouragement, which tries to deprive us of courage in life. These strongholds try to block us from making progress in life by erecting thought patterns of dismay and depression. In short, strongholds are thought patterns and modes of thinking which are satanically energized and built to keep us from being all that God created us to be."

A stronghold may involve weaknesses of the flesh such as improper sexual thoughts, addictive behaviors, fears, poor self-image, self-deprecation, and excessive self-criticism. In his book, *The Three Battlegrounds*, Francis Frangipane writes,

> If you want to identify the hidden strongholds in your life, you need only to survey the attitudes in your heart. Every area in your thinking that glistens with hope in God is an area which is being liberated by Christ. But any system of thinking that does not have hope, which feels hopeless, is a stronghold which must be pulled down. (*Advancing Church Pubs.*, 1989, p. 29).

We develop strongholds in our life mostly the following ways. These become patterns of thinking etched into our minds and the programs by which we operate:

1. A strong positive or negative experience.
2. Repetitive inputs, usually in the form of words from someone we love or trust.
3. Fear-based imaginations or thought patterns contrary to the Word of God which we habitually think upon until they become unconscious habits or aspects of our personalities.

4. Ideas, creeds, and belief systems we acquire from groups, organizations, or movements.
5. Perceptions and ideas instilled into us by the mass media.
6. Attitudes, beliefs, and practices passed on from generation to generation, by words and through modeled behavior.
7. Imaginations and thought patterns we have created ourselves, or have allowed our minds to generate as a reaction to outside forces.

A prime example of a stronghold which develops in someone's mind is the situation of a young child who is unwanted and poorly treated by his or her parents. This child does not get love and attention at the early age when it is needed. Its parents have not properly bonded with the child who begins, as a result, to feel insecure and unloved. This unloved feeling causes the child to question its self-worth and wonder what it is about him or her that is not worth loving. At this point, great harm can be done to the child emotionally and psychologically through a lack of proper parental love. In later years, this lack of love may manifest itself in addictive behaviors, which can become a love substitute; or a propensity for cults and authoritarian groups, which offer a counterfeit sense of belonging and family; or other destructive behaviors.

The root of the individual's problems is the strongholds developed through painful childhood experiences. Instead of being raised by loving parents, the child is raised by emotionally distant and uncaring parents.

Strongholds of self-doubt, poor self-image, fear, loneliness, and anger are created in the child's personality.

HOW TO DISMANTLE THE STRONGHOLDS IN YOUR LIFE

The only way to do this is to allow the Holy Spirit to identify the stronghold, and allow the Holy Spirit to dismantle it through forgiveness. Thus, a new personality based on God's total love and acceptance of the person is created, along with a new positive self-image. This does not usually happen, however, in a relational vacuum. God will bring individuals and substitute families into that person's life to help facilitate the healing process. Perhaps a local church will become the new family, a place where the healing process can begin for him or her.

The only way to dismantle a stronghold such as the false image of being a failure, or for that matter tearing down and uprooting any stronghold in our mind, is to do the following steps:

Step One: Identify the thoughts, ideas, perceptions, or inner belief systems which are in contradiction to what the Bible states about you. For example, if you keep thinking you are a failure, recognize that this is directly opposite to what God's Word says about you. "We are more than conquerors in Christ Jesus."

Step Two: Pray for God to dismantle the stronghold in your mind and keep on praying until the job is done.

Step Three: Pray and ask God to erect new and positive thought patterns in your mind that agree with what God says about you.

Step Four: Find out who you are in the Word of God and what God says about your life; then study and meditate on it until it goes deep within you.

Step Five: Do not talk fear, failure, or defeat. It is important to be honest and confess our sins to one another and ask for help in prayer. But we must also talk the language of what God's Word says about us and our lives.

Step Six: Recognize that warfare is involved and that the weapons of our warfare are not of the flesh, but are mighty through God to the pulling down of strongholds. Inner freedom and victory will often not come without spiritual warfare and continual battle.

Step Seven: The old computer programming expression says GIGO, or Garbage In, Garbage Out. What you program into your mind is what you will be. It is important to be part of a local church and participate, praise, and worship. Feed your mind and spirit with input that will edify you. Avoid as much as possible those people and circumstances which have a negative influence on you. Surround yourself with uplifting people and situations what will inspire and motivate you.

11

THE PRINCIPLE OF A RENEWED MIND

One of the primary results of the fall was on the psychological level. First, the consciousness of the existence and presence of God was lost, and second, there was a movement from a faith-based mentality toward a fear-based mentality. When mankind moved from faith to fear, a variety of evils came into the world.

The key then to living and practicing the principles of breakthrough is the renewal of our minds with God's Word. This can be called *The Principle of a Renewed Mind.* The basic concept is to learn how to think again the way Adam and Eve did in the Garden of Eden. There are four basic mind sets we must learn how to again develop.

1. Develop the capacity to live in the presence of
   God, not based on feelings, but faith.

2. Develop a faith-based mind set. Learn to perceive reality as God's Word teaches you to perceive it.

3. See ordinary reality and present-day situations from the point of view of the promises of God's Word.

4. Do not allow yourself to think just any pattern of thought that comes naturally. Constantly review your thought patterns and evaluate them in the light of God's Word. In other words, do these thoughts, ideas, and beliefs coincide with what God says? If they don't, then actively change the way you think to line up with God's Word.

12

GETTING TO KNOW GOD
AS HE REALLY IS

It is a sad fact that much of the human race is ignorant of the true nature of God and how great His power is. Because of that, they do not accept Christ as their Savior or walk in the ways of God. In Second Corinthians 4:3-4, the Apostle Paul says:

> And even if our gospel is veiled, it is veiled to those who are perishing, in whose case the god of this world has blinded the minds of the unbelieving, that they might not see the light of the gospel of the glory of Christ, who is the image of God (NAS).

We must understand that each of us exists in a world where there is a great conflict going on in an invisible or spiritual realm between the forces of God and the devil. It is the prime strategy of the devil to blind people to the reality and truth of the Gospel of Jesus Christ.

Most of the population of the United States does not really believe in the truth of the Gospel of Jesus Christ. The same is true, in fact, of most of the population of planet Earth. It is sad to know that in virtually every country people are blind to the mighty works of God and deaf to the healing power of His Word.

It is impossible to be all that we were created to be when we are in a state of deception or delusion. I have often been amazed when I have met gifted, brilliant, and creative people, and discover that they have been led astray by the false doctrines of this world. The root of the deception, however, is not intellectual but spiritual. They have been deceived ultimately, not by an ideology, but by a spirit behind the ideology.

However, another primary area of deception exists, and that is in the area of the Christian world itself. Many sincere Christians are completely unaware of the full meaning of salvation and the total reality of Christ. What we need is a modern Reformation, a return to what the Gospel of Jesus Christ really means.

The God of the Old and New Testament is the real God of the past and the future. He is beyond history and exists in eternity. But many Christians of our day do not have a real perception of who God is. They make Jesus Christ Lord only of the past rather than the Lord of all time and eternity. Thus, their presentation of the Gospel does not speak to today's realities, and it does not contain the truth and power necessary to transform the world. The true Gospel of Jesus Christ always transforms the individual and the world. It is revolutionary and life-changing. It is sane, powerful, integral, and radical, creating a real spiritual revolution against the tyranny of sin and darkness wherever it exists.

Many Christians are clinging to the past world—a world that no longer exists—as a kind of religious security blanket. This is reflected in the style and content of many current evangelical messages, which sound to our society as if the Gospel was being played on old and scratchy phonograph records while the god of this age cranks up his music of deception on compact discs. It is not the Gospel which is powerless to change America; the limitations we put on the Gospel make it of no effect.

Jesus Christ is the same, yesterday, today and forever! He understands life as it really is today and He has answers that can reach us where we are. Even as you read the pages of this book, the God of the universe is transmitting information into our spirits about how to solve life's problems, and answering our prayers. God is not asleep nor does He slumber. He is on the job. God is providing the solutions and provisions that each of us individually need. Even though sin and unbelief often prevent us from hearing God clearly, still the Holy Spirit is always with us, encouraging us to hear. When we do, we find that Jesus Christ has been sitting right next to us all the time, helping to carry our burdens and realize our dreams. The God of the Bible is fantastic, wonderful, and truly amazing. He defies description. The key is to realize who He really is, how powerful He is, and how much He wants to help us in our situations in life right now.

At this present moment, God is available to you. All He wants you to do is step into the stream of His presence. Step into the river of His blessing and allow the bubbling currents to carry you to your destiny. Does that mean you are not to participate and work? Of course not! But you must believe that God is truly on your side in life. God is not your enemy. God moves to help you when you ask Him to in prayer. If you could see into the invisible realm, you would observe that you are not alone. God and His angels are with you; supernatural power is available to help you right now. Let God step off the pages of your Bible and into your life. If He helped Joshua, Moses, Abraham, Paul, John, David, Daniel, Martha, and Mary, then He will help you.

Release your load and burden to the Lord. Allow Christ to dispel your fears. Let Jesus take the yoke of oppression off your back. Feel it being lifted right now. God didn't put it there. The devil used your fears and secret doubts to put you in slavery and bondage. But Jesus Christ just set you free. Now, in order to continue to walk in that freedom, you need to live in praise and worship of God. Allow your inner soul to rejoice in Him. Allow those streams of living water to bubble up from within. Jesus Christ said, "You shall know the truth and the truth shall set you free." You have a divine right to live in that freedom.

13

THE POWER OF A RENEWED MIND

We have seen that Adam and Eve lived in a powerful state of oneness with God where they were free to be everything they were created to be. It was a state of blessing and rich communion with the Creator of the universe. The Bible tells us that once you have received Christ as your Savior, you will "... not be conformed to this world, but be transformed by the renewing of your mind, that you may prove what the will of God is, that which is good and acceptable and perfect" (Rom. 12:2 NAS). In other words, it is God's plan for us to be completely whole, sinless, joyous, creative, and with plan and purpose.

The doorway into the kingdom of heaven is salvation. But the complete meaning of the word salvation implies more then just going to heaven. We need to renew our minds to learn how to think as powerful, whole, faith-filled, positive, dynamic, and loving people. One of the hallmarks of truly biblical Christians should be clarity and soundness of mind, producing power and purpose. Obviously, all of us are in the process of renewing our minds and are at different stages of the process. As such, we must have great compassion and love for those whom God has rescued from great psychological and spiritual destruction. Many people have been deeply hurt by what has happened to them in their lives. These people need our help and our prayers to lift them up. The goal of God is for each of us to cooperate with the Holy Spirit in the lifetime process of renewing our minds.

It is this mind-renewing process which allows the creative power of the Holy Spirit into our thought processes and inner chambers of our consciousness. This is part of God's plan for redemption. It is also part of what the word salvation means. God sent us His Son Jesus Christ, not to just save souls but rather to save people as people—completely unique individuals with their own personalities, memories, lives, and characteristics.

He came to save us as unique individuals with identity and purpose, not just as souls, but as real, complete people who have names like Jim, Sally, Dave, Kristina, Paul, and the like. Each of us have names, because God believes in people as individuals.

God wants to renew our minds individually. Our personalities, memories, choices, and lives are important to Him. He is our Heavenly Father who looks upon each one of us as sons and daughters. He wants to see us grow into all that we were created to be.

God's purpose is to set us free and release us to our infinite possibilities, which are beyond the scope of our wildest imaginations.

The Holy Spirit and the Word of God are at work to bring light to all dark areas of our minds, to cleanse us by the blood of Christ from the contaminating power of sin, to enable us to rethink our lives and purposes. But most of all, God is a loving Father who is doing everything in His power to help us be everything we can be.

The inference to be drawn is that God wants to change the way we think at all levels. He wants us to move from a fallen mind to a renewed one. Below is a list of the attributes of the fallen mind and the renewed mind.

THE FALLEN MIND	THE RENEWED MIND
Fear	Faith
Anxiety	Peace
Hate	Love
Purposelessness	Purpose
Powerlessness	Power
Confusion	Clearness
Dullness	Creativity
Victim	Non-victim
Low self-esteem	Strong self-esteem
Lust	Love
Taking	Giving
Seeking to be served	Serving
Irresponsible	Responsible
Compromising	Integrity
Addictive	Whole
Negative	Positive
Jealous	Empowering
Bitter	Thankful
Doubting	Trusting

Obviously, the list could go on and on, but the point is, God is in the process of renewing our minds. Our responsibility is to cooperate in the "Earth School Growth Program." The key to a renewed mind lies in understanding and practicing the new ways we should think. The purpose of God in our lives is to reprogram our minds completely so we can transcend this fear-consciousness and loss of God-consciousness that permeates the world system. God's power to enable us to do that is available to all of us right now.

14

YOU ARE UNDER CONSTRUCTION

Once you have accepted Jesus Christ into your life, God begins the process of building a brand new you! Through the power of His Holy Spirit, we become people who are under construction. When God created us, He had a good, positive, and creative plan in mind for what we would become. Due to various negative factors in this fallen world, however, most of us have failed to become all God had in mind for us.

The reason why we have so much anxiety, frustration, and anger in our lives is because we have a dream. Our relationships, our world, and that dream are blocked by various factors that seem to be outside of our control. We know what we could become and what our lives could be if we just had the power to make it all work. The tragedy is that our lives are often ripped apart by forces that we cannot control. All manner of misfortune seem to plague us incessantly.

In the midst of this chaos and confusion, Jesus Christ comes into our lives with heavenly purpose and power. There is no situation that is impossible for God to deal with, for He is in the business of taking broken and shattered lives and putting them back together.

All of us were raised by imperfect parents in an imperfect world. Some of us have experienced greater pain and suffering than others, and some of us have been abused emotionally and physically. All of us have experienced the pain and suffering of living in this fallen world.

In Los Angeles, we recently went through one of our city's greatest tragedies. After the Rodney King trial, Los Angeles became a city under siege. Beatings, burnings, and looting occurred on an unprecedented scale. The National Guard had to be sent in to restore order. What happened in Los Angeles was a microcosm of what happens in people's lives everywhere when they are crushed by forces of hatred and injustice. Most of the people who did the looting and the burning were hopeless and desperate people. Their lives were the products of dysfunctional homes, racism, poverty, and the violence of living in the urban ghetto. What they did was wrong, but it is clear that wrongs were done to a people and to a culture. The cycle of sin and evil was at work, damaging families and individual lives.

Injustice produces bitterness, which in turn produces hatred and violence. Hatred and violence produce racism, and racism produces injustice. Black, White, Latino, Asian—all people alike—miss God's plan for their lives when they react, rather than act according to His Word.

All of this was tragic, but none of it was God's will. God has a far better plan for our lives. It was never God's intention that people live in the despair of emotional or material poverty! Hopelessness does not come from God; it is a form of spiritual darkness. God has a plan for people's lives to become all that He created them to become. He has given the human race amazing talents and abilities. Every living person has received tremendous gifts and great potential from God. Throughout the Bible, God is depicted as a God of fruitfulness. He gives power to the weak. He heals the sick. He is a good God!

But the problem is that sin and evil come to thwart the work of God. In this life there is intense spiritual conflict between good and evil. Nevertheless, if we will believe that God really is a good God and partner with Him in His plan, then amazing things can happen in our lives. Despair and hopelessness are driven away by the glorious entrance of God's Word.

What happened in Los Angeles can happen in our own lives if we do not know the reality of God's power and promises. Ultimately, the Los Angeles gangs, and anyone guilty of racism, have been deceived by the powers of darkness. Such groups, or people, are led to believe the only way to get ahead is by suppressing others and using force. They are blind to the reality of God's existence and His power.

This can also happen in our individual lives. We can become overwhelmed by our problems and miss the entrance to God's delivering kingdom. No matter the wreck our lives have become, we can be rebuilt by God's power. But we must read His blueprint in His Word and cooperate with His Holy Spirit.

This was my experience. I was vainly searching for answers and getting frustrated because I could not find them. However, God in His love for me sent people into my life to tell me about Jesus Christ. After a great deal of resistance, I finally accepted Christ into my life and found the answers I was looking for.

I realized that God really existed, that He loved me, and had a plan for my life beyond pain and suffering. I began to read the promises of God in His Word. This allowed the Holy Spirit to change my negative attitudes and perceptions about life that had been formed during an unhappy childhood and then reinforced by a fallen society.

I became a person under construction by the Holy Spirit, and a brand new me was being built. Layer after layer of pain and sadness was being removed while God was rebuilding me from the inside. He began to reshape my thought patterns and ideas about who I was and what life was all about.

I discovered firsthand what a marvelous adventure life can become when we let God direct our paths. I understood that God loved me, and only wanted me to be everything I was created to be. He therefore sent His power into my life to make it happen. God did not just dangle wonderful promises before me to tease me and then say, "Go ahead and struggle, boy, and maybe you can realize your dreams." No! Instead, God said, "Look at these wonderful dreams I have for you, Paul. They are going to be yours and I am going to give you My power, My resources, and My strength to make it happen."

15

REBUILDING YOU

God is not only the Creator of the universe, but also the architect of a brand new you. After you have accepted Jesus Christ, you are in the process of rebuilding. The Holy Spirit is actively at work in you to transform you.

Each of us is a fallen creature, and it is only through the powerful work of Jesus Christ that we are being molded and shaped into new creatures in Him. Those are not empty words. God has an incredible blueprint for your new personality. The message of Jesus Christ is about all of life.

When the Apostle Paul said, "I pray that the eyes of your heart may be enlightened, so that you may know what is the hope of His calling, what are the riches of the glory of His inheritance in the saints," he was talking about how awesome is your eternal destiny, which begins here on Earth.

The very God of the universe is reconstructing a chosen race of people to inherit eternity to rule and reign with Him forever. No matter how dismal your present state of affairs, if you are in Christ you are being prepared and rebuilt to become one of the inheritors of a marvelous cosmic destiny. This destiny begins right where you are now, and if you cooperate with the Holy Spirit, you will reign in the affairs of this life through Him.

God delights in taking people off the garbage dumps of life and fashioning them into princes and princesses. His wonderful power is available to rebuild us into a people after His design. You are a work under construction, a masterpiece in the making.

Jesus Christ is transforming us for the time when we will literally step through the doors of infinity and have the universe placed in our hands as a gift. What this means is that our bodies and minds are going to be completely transformed. All physical defects will be gone and our bodies will radiate with divine perfection. Our minds will take a quantum leap in intelligence, and we will have powers we never dreamed of. All creation is going to explode violently with a brilliance and awesome beauty that is only hinted at here on earth with scenes of mountains, waterfalls, and sunsets.

Your personality is going to change radically, and in an instant you will become everything good you ever dreamed you could become. All of your relationships with other people will be infinite, rich, joyous, and eternal. You will experience the most wondrous and massive life change possible. You are going to shed mortality and put on immortality. You are going to know what it means to be in Christ, Him who will be set on the throne to be worshipped for evermore.

This present reality is just for a moment and, though you may have experienced great pain and suffering, you are being groomed for an important role in heaven. Once you have accepted Christ, the Holy Spirit's power begins rebuilding your being and personality and redeeming you from the curse.

It's like being a pauper, clothed in rags all your life, having to go around and beg. Then one day someone comes to you and tells you that you are no longer a beggar, that you have inherited a kingdom, and you can become a prince or princess if you will choose to accept it.

When this happens to you—and it will!—a difficult transition from beggar to becoming royalty will ensue. But this is exactly what has happened to you in Christ. At that moment, you will start being transformed by God for a great destiny.

GETTING REAL

It is easy to say that we are sons and daughters of God, or that we are joint-heirs with Jesus Christ. But the question should naturally be asked, "What does all that have to do with the real world?" I hear a lot of people on TV talk big about God's miracle power, and I frankly wonder how well they would do out from under the bright lights of television!

All this talk of Christ and sitting at the right hand of the Father can be so much theological jargon unless it translates down to where I live. Fortunately, I have discovered that God's promises work right where I'm at, in the combat trenches of life.

More often than not, God's blessing reveals itself as you tough it out, work it out, and pray it through in the real world. Real partnership with God happens on the freeway, in the kitchen, while you're playing with your kids, or on your job. God's miracles reveal themselves in unexpected ways as we live our lives in expectation of His goodness. Miracles are not always instantaneous; but as the seasons pass and time progresses, it becomes very clear that He is moving powerfully on your behalf. This will happen in your life if you open yourself to God's power.

16

UNDERSTANDING
YOUR LIFE PROGRAMS

The Bible says, "Raise up a child in the way he should go and when he is old, he will not depart from it." The idea is that it is the responsibility of parents to train or program children in the right way to live. However, this principle could be taken a step further. Children learn through modeling their parents' behaviors, beliefs, and life styles.

Recently, I was talking to a man who was a homosexual. He knew that I was not only heterosexual, but "morally straight." He made a joke and then said, "Your marriage must make Ward and June Cleaver look conservative!" In his eyes, a fulfilled heterosexual marriage was a throwback to the Cleavers in *Leave it To Beaver*.

Just as children are programmed to accept certain life styles, so the culture at large can be programmed to move in a particular direction. Since the 1950s, the number of traditional nuclear families has gone into a sharp decline and the number of single-parent families has risen. More and more children are growing up with only one parent to look to for guidance and support. Many couples are deciding to live together without getting married. Currently, one out of every four children is born out of wedlock. Abortions are now becoming increasingly common. Statisticians have also noted an increase in teenage drug and alcohol abuse and—more tragically —suicide.

The bottom line is that many people are no longer raised in homes with both parents who love them. This, and what is termed the dysfunctional family, has created a society where millions of people are now raised in unhappy circumstances. The net effect of these new trends is that such people are no longer being raised by loving parents. They are therefore growing up with a tremendous loss of self-esteem, poor self-images, negative role models for marriage, an inability to develop healthy relationships, loneliness, and addiction disorders.

Both my wife Kristina and I understand a great deal of this. I was raised in a home split by divorce. My father had left home by the time I was just entering puberty. There was alcoholism in the home. Kristina also experienced a loss of relationships in a dysfunctional home due to alcoholism. Both of us were programmed for conflict and divorce. Even though we were Christians, the simple act of marriage to each other did nothing to eliminate the likelihood of marital failure.

You cannot put two such people together in marriage and then just automatically expect the marriage to work. What Kristina and I needed—and what millions of people need—was a completely new program input into our minds and souls. Second Corinthians 5:17 says, "Therefore if any man is in Christ, he is a new creature; the old things passed away; behold, new things have come (Or, all things have become new)." This is a powerful promise from God that says, *You don't have to be stuck in your old negative habits and life programs! I have the power to totally transform and change your life!*

It doesn't do a whole lot of good to tell people they have inner problems. Most of them know this. Most have been trying for years to wrestle free of such problems, but for them, it's like trying to struggle free of quicksand. The more they struggle, the deeper they sink! Jesus Christ can do what self-help manuals and therapy do not have sufficient power to do, and that is to create a sparkling new you and a sparkling new life for you that will transcend your wildest dreams!

I understand the power of Jesus Christ to change a life on a personal level. About twenty years ago, after years of psychotherapy, Eastern meditation, Zen Buddhism, Hinduism, consciousness expansion, reality and Gestalt therapy, hypnosis, philosophy study, yoga, LSD experimentation, and an entire gamut of New Age and mind science disciplines, I still saw no way out of my emotional problems. No way out, that is, but suicide. However, my life was miraculously spared, and eventually I surrendered it to Jesus Christ. Then I began to experience powerful psychological and spiritual healing in my personality. When I confessed my sins to Jesus Christ and was cleansed by His blood, a power change occurred in my being. Up to then, I didn't even believe in the word sin. Still, I felt purified and forgiven when I invited Christ into my life and became a new creation!

Up until that time, I had been programmed to self-destruct. Some of these programs, or strongholds, are listed below:

PROGRAMS

1. Inability to conceive of, or believe in, a happy marriage.
2. Belief in resolving conflicts through arguing in a negative and destructive manner.
3. A victim, or "poor me," consciousness.
4. Self-doubt and insecurity.
5. A subconscious desire to destroy my marriage, because a happy marriage was outside of my inner belief system, or comfort zone.
6. A poverty or failure consciousness fostering the belief that I must always struggle and didn't deserve good things in life.
7. Fear of having children, because the task of raising them was viewed as burdensome and expensive.
8. Fear of sexual boredom because "monogamy was monotony."
9. Depression and anxiety—not joy and happiness —were normal. Normal was being unhappy.
10. A fear-based consciousness: fear of life, fear of fun, fear of success, fear of death, fear of sickness, fear of everything.
11. Failure consciousness: my inner belief system taught me that failure was my destiny.

The result of this negative programming is that during our courtship, and soon after Kristina and I were married, a series of intense conflicts erupted in our relationship. These conflicts were rooted in strongholds that had been built into us over a lifetime of being raised in dysfunctional homes. Thus, even though we were madly in love, we repeatedly fought like cats and dogs. It got so bad that we almost divorced.

This was an intensely frustrating experience, because we both loved God, prayed, and went to church. Nonetheless, these inexplicable forces would explode into our lives almost as if we were an airplane flying into a storm on auto-pilot. It took me years to understand that these conflicts stemmed from the strongholds, or programs, with which we were raised. It was as if we went into marriage, both burdened with many large suitcases of emotional baggage that were certain, sooner or later, to drag us down and destroy us.

Slowly, through prayer and commitment, we struggled towards wholeness. Thus we gradually molded into a harmonious relationship of beauty and love. But the process took far longer than it should have, because there was no one there to show us the way. In addition, we felt an intense guilt for our failure. After all, we thought, "If we were really committed Christians, then all of this would not have been happening."

THE HOLY SPIRIT—GOD'S PSYCHIATRIST

Very slowly though, the puzzle pieces came together. The Holy Spirit began to shed light on the programming in our memory banks, and the negative experiences that had shaped our childhoods. We began to realize that:

The weapons of our warfare are not of the flesh, but divinely powerful for the destruction of fortresses (strongholds or programs). We are destroying speculations (strongholds, programs, negative memories) and every lofty thing raised up against the knowledge of God, and we are taking every thought captive to the obedience of Christ (2 Cor. 10: 4-5).

The key to breakthrough is to allow the Holy Spirit to identify the strongholds, or programs in our lives which block us from being all God created us to be. Plus, we need to cooperate with the Holy Spirit in letting Him destroy those negative programs. But then we must go one step further. We must allow the Creator to establish brand new programs in our personalities and relationships by renewing our minds to what the Word of God says about us. The result will always be a new birth of hope and promise for our lives and the way of new creation.

The whole process can be likened to a huge painting in one's mind. Destructive experiences paint dark and ominous portraits on the canvas of our lives. Then a Master Artist comes along and wipes the pain and suffering from the picture. Then He begins to paint a wonderful masterpiece of life and color. The more we trust this Master Artist, the more He creates a picture that is magnificent and priceless. In addition, as a skilled painter He actually transforms the negative images and colors into things of great beauty. That is what God wants to do in our lives.

17

HOW TO GET RID OF YOUR
MENTAL BLOCK AND SUCCEED:
OVERCOMING FEAR AND FAILURE

Could it be possible that you actually have a mental block against success? Is it possible that you still have a slave mentality and have actually grown used to failure, depression, chaos, marital discord, broken dreams, panic, and lack of career fulfillment? Sometimes we are afraid of genuine breakthrough because it will mean change and charting a new course into the unknown.

In order to move into the place of blessing God has for you, the abundant life, you must recognize that you have some strongholds in your life against success, fulfillment, happiness, and peace. It may sound a little strange, but if you are used to being a victim, you may find the prospect of *not* being a victim a bit frightening.

We must understand that the enemy may have erected strongholds in our lives through our upbringing and other environmental factors. The fact is, we may actually have what could be referred to as a ghetto mentality.

What is a ghetto mentality? Research has shown that many times, even after leaving the slums, people cannot get *rid* of their old attitudes. Research further shows that where modern housing developments have been built for such people, their ghetto mentalities have caused them to destroy their new homes within a year after they have moved in. The reason for this is that even though you may change a person's outside environment, it will not do much good unless there is a corresponding change on the inside. Along with improving external physical structures, the human mind must be rebuilt as well.

This explains why so many people from dysfunctional homes continue to have problems after they leave those homes and start their own families. It is also the reason why children of alcoholics marry alcoholics, or other adult children of alcoholics. Both are examples of seeking sameness and familiarity, even if that sameness and familiarity are destructive.

Fortunately, there is an answer. God has given us the power to engraft new modes of thinking upon our human consciousness through the Word of God, prayer, and the power of the Holy Spirit. You have been given the power to break the slave mentality and remove your mental block against success through the creative power of God's Holy Spirit.

This entails allowing God to write a new consciousness based on the promises of His Word upon your inner man or woman. The way this happens is that you begin to read, study, and meditate upon the Word of God and, as you do, the energizing and powerful force of God's living Word begins to regenerate and recreate your inner being so that old things pass away, and all things become new.

> For the word of God is living and active and sharper than any two-edged sword, and piercing as far as the division of soul and spirit, of both joints and marrow, and able to judge the thoughts and intentions of the heart (Heb. 4:12).

This promise of God tells us that God's Word is actual, living energy. In fact, God's Word is God himself going into our inner being and recreating it. "In the beginning was the Word, and the Word was with God, and the Word was God" (John 1:1). In Genesis 1:1, it says, "In the beginning God created the heavens and the earth," and a little later on it says, "And God created man in His own image." God is a Creator and a Master Designer with the power to recreate your personality so that you are made whole. His creative power is in the Holy Spirit and His Word.

There is a powerful principle at work in the human personality which yields itself to the entrance of light from the kingdom of God. Not only can a person be forgiven and restored, but God can recreate memories, mind, and imagination.

For example, the fearful person can be made bold and positive. The insecure person can be made secure. Someone who is a homosexual can become attracted to the opposite sex. The addict can find deliverance from his addiction. The power of God is able to recreate the human personality to an incredible extent. Not only can you get rid of your mental block against success and learn to overcome your fear of failure, but there are provisions from the kingdom of God that will enable you to live in a new place of power, position, and authority. Remember, you who are in Christ are now sitting with Him in the invisible realm at the right hand of the Father in heavenly places. Ephesians 1:19-20:

> And what is the surpassing greatness of His power toward us who believe. These are in accordance with the working of the strength of His might which He brought about in Christ, when He raised Him from the dead, and seated Him at His right hand in the heavenly places.

Spiritually, you are seated with Christ at the right hand of the Father as an inheritor, due to the death and resurrection of Jesus Christ. Once you have invited Christ into your life, then you are a joint-heir with Him. As such, you are going to rule and reign with Him for eternity. At this moment you are already in a position of reigning, and this present Earth School is like a graduate course you must take before getting your degree. It's not that you are earning salvation, because you're not. Salvation and your inheritance are a free gift, because you are with Christ. But you can grow in grace and the knowledge of God where you learn to live and use your kingdom authority.

Thus, in your inner being, you are already victorious and ruling. The difficulty is that you must learn to renew your mind to eternal truth which is one of the reasons you must go through Earth School to educate your human spirit, mind, and body. The problems you face are not due to the Holy Spirit within you, but to a need for educating and growing the mind.

As I write these words, my eight-month-old son is playing on the carpet beneath me gurgling baby words. As a parent, I can envision the future and see him as an adult. The day will come when he is capable of walking, talking, and making adult decisions. As a loving father who has been given this gift of a child, my job is to guide him to adulthood the same way the Holy Spirit is guiding us today to spiritual adulthood. And just as my baby boy has the seeds of adulthood within him as well as God-given gifts and potentials, so has God placed in all of us treasures that will be released as we grow in Him.

YOU ARE DESTINED TO SUCCEED

Is success in life a matter of luck and chance? Do some people succeed because they have the right education and social background? It is true that these attributes, plus good timing, all play a role in a person's ability to prosper in life. The ultimate factor in success, though, is not luck, education or background, but CHOICE. In order for people to succeed, they must first *choose* to succeed.

It is true that environmental factors have a great impact on a person's life. But there have been plenty of people born to wealth and education who have been dismal failures, as well as scores of people who have risen from poverty to impressive success. The overriding factor is the inner will to make a personal commitment to success.

Thus we come to the *First Principle of Success*: *success is a matter of choice*. In order to succeed in life, you must decide to succeed. You must commit to the accomplishment of your goals no matter what the cost. Once you make this commitment, amazing things will begin to happen. Your life will begin to be on course. You will know where you are going. You will be on target and you will hit your mark.

In order to achieve the true goal of success, you must have the proper definition of what success truly is. *Webster's New Collegiate Dictionary* defines the word "succeed" in several ways, but the one which applies here is 2b: to attain a desired object or end.

Among many synonyms for *succeed* are *prosper, thrive,* and *flourish*. One of Webster's definitions for the word *success* is the attainment of wealth, favor, or eminence. These are the classic definitions of the word, yet they encompass only a partial understanding of its true meaning.

To really understand this concept, we must first realize that true success transcends the material and physical realm and engages the spiritual one. You may well ask, "What does spirituality have to do with success?" The answer, of course, is everything! To understand success in life, we must first understand life and its purpose; otherwise, we will find it impossible to reach our goals in life. If we do not understand these true goals, we cannot succeed.

The only way to understand success is to know that man is a triune being. He is made up of three parts: body, soul, and spirit. The body is the physical part—the heart, flesh, eyes, and skin. The soul is the emotional and intellectual part—our thoughts, feelings, and memories. Finally, a person's spirit is his eternal part, the part that lives forever. In order to succeed in life, one must prosper in all three areas, not just one or two.

Jesus Christ talked about this when He said, "For what does it profit a man to gain the whole world, and forfeit his soul?" (Mark 8:36 NAS). To put it another way, "What good does it do to be rich and famous if you are spiritually bankrupt?" The world is full of examples of people who have had it all but were spiritually poor. There are countless stories of people who "made it" but, because they did not succeed spiritually, their "success" was empty. Life's great lesson is that money, riches, sex, and fame do not, in and of themselves, bring happiness. For many, this lesson must be learned, by experience, over and over again.

The *Second Principle of Success* then is *in order to succeed, you must first have the proper definition of success*. If you think success is just a matter of power, sex, money, and fame, then you are going to end up bankrupt in life. The Bible has this to say about success, "Beloved, I wish above all things that thou mayest prosper and be in health, even as thy soul prospereth" (3 John 2 KJV).

The very Creator of the universe wants us to prosper beyond our wildest dreams, but He wants us to have the right idea about success. True prosperity can only happen to you as long as your soul prospers.

18

DEVELOPING AN EXPANDED
DEFINITION OF SUCCESS

No one would deny that in America today there are many ideas about what it means to succeed. In general, the accumulation of wealth and power is thought to mean that a person has achieved success. Many people will stop at nothing in order to get enough money to buy bigger houses, expensive cars, memberships in exclusive country clubs, and the like.

Many Christians too regard the accumulation of such status symbols as the way to achieve success, happiness, and fulfillment. But disappointment and disillusionment are often the only results. Christians can also be hampered by the belief that God is against success.

GOD WANTS YOU TO SUCCEED

The idea that God wants you to succeed is a radical concept for many people. It is true that some people are called to live lives of persecution, hardship, or even martyrdom. In fact, anyone who chooses to go against the flow of a society that has rejected its spiritual foundations is going to experience these things to some degree. However, not everyone is called to be like Mother Teresa and go to India, or to become a missionary in some far-off land.

Many of us were chosen to be sales people, businessmen, housewives, athletes, artists, or truck drivers. There are plenty of opportunities to be missionaries and feed the poor from out of the context of our daily lives. However, from God's perspective, there is no such thing as an ordinary life.

The key to understanding true success in life is to travel back to the beginning of time to see what the Creator had in mind for mankind in Adam and Eve, the original models for life on Earth .

Travel through time is, of course, merely the stuff of science fiction. But were we to travel back in time today, we would get a glimpse of what God's plan was for mankind. We were originally created to live in eternity.

Traveling back thousands and thousands of years by jumping into a time machine would allow us a glimpse of this planet we call Earth when it was truly a paradise. God's original plan was for mankind to live in total paradise with glowing sunsets, waterfalls, rainbows, flowers, and endless joy and happiness in an intimate relationship with Him.

In Genesis 1:28, it says, "And God blessed them; and God said to them, 'Be fruitful and multiply, and fill the earth, and subdue it; and rule over the fish of the sea and over the birds of the sky, and over every living thing that moves on earth.'" God gave Adam and Eve a perfect world and told them to have dominion over it. This leads to the ***Third Principle of Success:*** *dominion.*

The implication of mankind having dominion over planet Earth was that there were to be no such things as poverty, sickness, diseases, or any other similar problems. People were to live totally successful lives with mastery over their environment. But it didn't turn out that way.

How we lost mastery over our world, along with our personal power, becomes the key question. The answer can be summed up in one word—disobedience. Adam and Eve did not obey one commandment of God: "From the tree of the knowledge of good and evil you shall not eat, for in the day that you eat from it you shall surely die" (Gen. 2: 17).

It was not a difficult commandment to obey. God said, "Look, I have given you this wonderful place in which to live; go ahead and enjoy it forever. Just don't blow the whole thing by eating the fruit of that tree, because there is something deadly about it." This was completely reasonable. God was warning them about something dangerous; Adam and Eve should have heeded that warning.

But Adam and Eve did not listen. They were tempted by the force of evil in the form of a serpent to disobey God's clear instructions. Then all mankind's troubles began.

Death entered the human race, along with the full fury of its destructive power. Adam and Eve were forced to leave the Garden of Eden. Yet God—who is love—did not give up on the human race. God had a master plan for man and woman to return to Him. First, He sent His law in the form of the commandments to teach the human race how to please Him and how to live well. He used the Jewish race as the torchbearers of His eternal laws.

Second, He was preparing the human race for an awesome and powerful event that would reverse the curse. In the fullness of time, God sent His only Son Jesus Christ to die on a cross and be resurrected from the dead.

God's purpose for doing this was to break the power of sin over the human race. When Christ died on the cross, He took all of mankind's sin upon himself. This is why other spiritual teachings, no matter how noble, just don't complete the job of getting rid of sin. It was only Jesus Christ who overcame the destructive power of sin and death by dying and rising again from the dead.

Adam and Eve chose to disobey God and partake of the forbidden fruit. But you and I must accept Jesus Christ by faith. This is what the Bible means by being born again. We must choose to allow God's life force to come back into us. Remember the *First Principle of Success: success is a matter of choice.* We must therefore also choose to receive eternal life in Jesus Christ.

The acceptance of Christ into our lives activates His power within our beings so we can prosper in spirit, thereby freeing us to enjoy prosperity in other areas as well. We regain our authority and dominion and are in a position to rule in the affairs of life.

Does this free us from problems, difficulties, and life's inevitable challenges? No. Life is going to be difficult because we live in a fallen world. But when we accept Jesus Christ, He gives us the power to triumph over adversity. The choice is ours.

19

YOUR PERSONAL ROAD MAP
TO SUCCESS

As we discussed earlier, understanding your world view is crucial to your success in life. In the final analysis, Christianity is truth. The Bible is true scientifically, historically, and sociologically, as well as spiritually, regardless of whether or not you and I choose to believe in it. That Jesus Christ rose from the dead is historical fact, regardless of whether or not people choose to accept it.

Real reality, or final truth, tells us that we live in a supernatural universe that is ruled over by a personal, living God. He has not left us as orphans to attempt to carry on our lives without help. He has given us His Word, a clear set of instructions on how to live. This Word of God, the Bible, speaks to us in the nitty-gritty details of our lives. It talks to us about sex, money, hate, war, pollution, greed, love, marriage, careers, goals, and guidance. It is a real book about real issues.

In Psalm 19:7-13, David writes:

> The law of the Lord is perfect, restoring the soul;
> The testimony of the Lord is sure, making wise
>   the simple.
> The precepts of the Lord are right, rejoicing the
>   heart;
> The commandment of the Lord is pure,
>   enlightening the eyes.
> The fear of the Lord is clean, enduring forever;
> The judgments of the Lord are true; they are
>   righteous altogether.
> They are more desirable than gold, yes than
>   much fine gold;
> Sweeter also than honey and the drippings of the
>   honeycomb.
> Moreover, by them Thy servant is warned;
> In keeping them there is great reward.
> Who can discern his errors? Acquit me of
>   hidden faults.
> Also keep back Thy servant from presumptuous
>   sins;
> Let them not rule over me;
> Then I shall be blameless,
> And I shall be acquitted of great transgression.

The Bible is not just a collection of human words. The Word of God is an actual "lamp unto our feet." It lights our way in life. The person who properly utilizes the power of God's Word in his life is going to have an advantage over the person who walks in darkness. God has secrets that He only shares with those who walk in intimate relationship with Him and stay close to His Word.

If we take time to renew our minds with God's Word, we are going to have a much clearer perspective on every detail of our lives. We are going to gain God's perspective on matters. We are going to have discernment that comes from a higher source regarding situations and people. We are going to have an amplified intelligence and a supernatural understanding of the affairs of life that far transcends our merely human intellects.

All of us have a great capacity for foolishness and stupidity. By nature we are a people who—if left to our natural inclinations—would often choose to go down roads that lead to destruction. But when we allow God's Word into our lives, we are cleansed and restored from hidden faults and sins. The Word of God goes down into our inner beings, cleanses us, and fills us with light.

Being filled with God's light through the power of His Word has many practical benefits. We find that we no longer in struggle, but we begin to move into what the Bible calls a state of blessing.

When we live and operate in a state of blessing, it means that God's power to perform good in our lives overshadows us. When people look at our lives, they might at first glance think that we are "lucky," because even though we may have adversities and setbacks, things usually turn out all right for us. However, if they looked closer at our lives, they would see that we are not "lucky," but blessed. They would understand that there is a specific source of our good fortune and that source is God. God demonstrates His goodness to people through the lives of those He blesses.

THE KEY TO MIRACLES

Why is one person a success and another a failure? Is it money, education, or background? While these are important factors in producing a successful life, there is, however, something powerful and far more important than these characteristics. Many people have all these advantages but, nonetheless, their lives are disasters. There are many also who come from both financially and spiritually impoverished backgrounds, but who have become very successful.

A person's inner belief system, spiritually or even psychologically, releases power to accomplish great things. Such attitudes as bitterness, unbelief, doubt, cynicism, despair, or a failure consciousness close us off from the working of God's power. When we walk before God in praise, worship, and openness to His divine power, we can experience the flow of His kingdom power through us.

Satan's strategy is to imprison us within our own belief systems. Sin, disappointment, unfortunate experiences, and even fatigue help to build a wall between us and God's power. Otherwise well-meaning ministers and Christians, if they have had unhappy experiences in life, can begin to develop a mentality of failure and cynicism built on these negative experiences.

Our childlike faith is diminished and a genuine openness to miracles disappears. What is needed is a fresh turn from negativity and defeat, followed by a cleansing of the mind and soul with the blood of Jesus Christ. We then need to be open to the possibility of God's miracle power in a posture of praise and worship of the King. Not only will our lives be transformed but also those of the people and communities around us.

The danger is, we can become battle-weary without realizing it. Subtly, imperceptibly, our consciousness changes and our childlike capacity to believe in miracles diminishes. This is a mental stronghold from which we can be set free by allowing the Holy Spirit to renew our minds and fill us with the divine seeds of miracles.

If we allow this divine regeneration, a powerful spiritual revolution will happen inside us, completely transforming our lives and the lives of those around us. A supernatural power from heaven will be activated, and we will be literally charged with power. This means that, despite the sea of emotions that passes through us, we will draw on the wellsprings of life from the throne of God.

20

WORDS THAT CREATE STRONGHOLDS

We must be extremely careful what we say to friends, children, spouses, co-workers, and neighbors. Words can either set people free or imprison them. Jesus Christ said, "And I say to you, that every careless word that men shall speak, they shall render account for it on the day of judgment." That was not just a passing remark. Jesus was telling us that our words have power to change the destiny of lives and nations for good or evil.

Some people think Jesus was warning us against the use of profanity, but the truth goes a lot deeper than that. Every time we make a remark about somebody, we are actually doing something powerful to their perception of reality. Think of the power the words of a parent or teacher can have on young, impressionable children. One careless remark about a child's abilities, looks, or intelligence can affect them for a lifetime. People have literally chosen careers after one remark made to them such as, "My! Aren't you good with numbers!" or music, or whatever. By the same token, a remark like, "You really aren't very bright!" can possibly destroy a potential future.

Our words can set free, empower, or imprison and place in bondage. Even as I write these words I can sense the convicting power of the Holy Spirit in my own life. Like many others, I am often guilty of speaking too casually or glibly. I need God's forgiveness and His Lordship over my tongue.

I can remember some of the seemingly innocent remarks people made to me in passing, remarks that placed me in tremendous bondage for years. I distinctly remember being in a car with a sincere Christian brother, with whom I was sharing my inner pain, when he blurted out, "It seems as though as long as I've known you, you've been trying to get your life together." I am sure it was a completely innocent remark on his part, yet it pressed the hot buttons of my personality and keyed into the deep fears and insecurities I had about my life.

His words plagued me for years and no doubt helped to bring about my very unorthodox career. I went from being an independent feature film producer, author, sales manager, and public relations director to a variety of other jobs. There was a lot of door-knocking and pavement pounding as I struggled to find my way in life. Those casual words would loom up from my memory to set off a whole range of fears and insecurities that I had a terrible time dealing with.

The point is, all of us have been affected powerfully by the remarks of others, positively or negatively. We need to speak blessings to people and allow the Holy Spirit to use us to create life in others. Perhaps you can remember a comment someone made in your life that freed you. Such words of encouragement can keep you going for a long time in life.

A single unkind sentence can place people in strongholds that diminish their capacity to become all that they were created to be. In the same way, if we learn to speak the truth in love and speak blessing on people, we can edify and uplift them. This means saying the right thing at the right time with anointing and wisdom.

WORDS CAN FREE OR IMPRISON

The power of the spoken word is of the utmost importance in understanding the generational curse. Through words or language, both blessings and curses can be passed on from one generation to another, for God has placed in our mouths the power to bless or curse others.

Little phrases such as, "I have my father's temper," or "everybody in our family gets headaches," are far more than merely idle words. They actually program people and can create the very negative situation they proclaim.

Conversely, repeated phrases that are positive, such as, "Everybody in our family knows how to make money," can actually create the mind set and predisposition to produce wealth. Words frame our consciousness and set boundaries and programs in our minds. We are not talking about superstitious repetition of words, but rather a correct understanding of the power in the words God has given us.

James 3:8-10 says:

> But no one can tame the tongue; it is a restless evil and full of deadly poison. With it we bless our Lord and Father; and with it we curse men, who have been made in the likeness of God; from the same mouth come both blessing and cursing. My brethren, these things ought not to be this way.

The Bible is not just talking about using profanity or bad-mouthing people. God has given us the power to build and destroy with our mouths. All of us have experienced on numerous occasions the absolutely devastating effect a person's words can have on us. Sometimes the negative things people say to us can create psychological bondage for years, placing powerful, negative strongholds in our minds that the enemy can use to limit and torment us with fear.

I know a man who was told by his parents and relatives while he was growing up how stupid he was, and he developed a horrible inferiority complex. Proverbs 18:21 states: "Death and life are in the power of the tongue." As Christians we need to learn the awesome responsibility of our words. God is going to hold us responsible for our words as well as our actions. Careless words can destroy lives, block the progress of ministries, and imprison people. On the other hand, words of blessing and encouragement can heal, restore, build, and release people and ministries.

Jesus Christ taught us in Matthew 12:35-37, "The good man out of his good treasure brings forth what is good;

and the evil man out of his evil treasure brings forth what is evil. And I say to you, that every careless word that men shall speak, they shall render account for it in the day of judgment. For by your words you shall be justified, and by your words you shall be condemned." The Lord makes it very clear that we are going to have to account for all of our words here on Earth.

Rev. Jack Hayford talks about the importance of telling people things that will build them up. He says most Christians fear doing this because they are afraid this will inflate egos and make people proud. Yet, Rev. Hayford goes on to share that, in all his years in the ministry, he has observed that most people do not suffer from pride.

Instead, the majority have tremendous doubts concerning their lives, and ministries desperately need to encourage, affirm, and bless people with their words. I can think of three distinct occasions at The Church On The Way when I was tremendously encouraged because of what people said to me.

Rev. Scott Bauer once walked up to me during a service and, placing his hand on my shoulder, said, "You are important to the Body of Christ."

On another occasion, Keith Dawson, director of the church's Living Way Bookstore, encouraged me concerning my first book, which had just been published.

Finally, while my wife Kristina and I were meeting with Pastor Jack Hayford, he told me how much he appreciated hearing a tape of a talk I had given.

Such words were medicine to my soul—simple words of encouragement that blessed and empowered me to go on. Far from making me egotistical, they gave me hope and encouragement. When trying any endeavor, sheer loneliness might tempt you to give up; but real words of encouragement can keep you going.

As friends, parents, leaders, and co-workers, we need to learn how to really bless people with our words. Satanic strongholds in peoples' lives can come tumbling down and people can be set free by the power of our words.

In Proverbs 25:11, "Like apples of gold in settings of silver is a word spoken in right circumstances." God has placed creative power in our tongues and a flow of healing and blessing can be released by our words. The spiritual atmosphere of homes, churches, and businesses can be changed by words, along with the direction of lives.

The generational curse is often passed on and created by words. However, words can just as well be used to not only break the curse, but to invoke and create blessing instead. This is why it is so important to read the Word of God and confess what the Bible says and God's promises out loud. By speaking God's Word and His blessing, we release the kingdom of God in our midst and drive out the power of hell.

21

OVERCOMING STRONGHOLDS IN MY LIFE

I became fascinated with the reality of strongholds in our lives because I have had to overcome so many of my own. Both my wife and I came from homes where alcoholism exerted a malign influence in the family. Even though we both have loving and generous parents—who have begun their own recovery and spiritual journey— our upbringing was with the habits engendered in dysfunctional households. In our cases, these roots are in the generational curse of alcoholism. As a result, strongholds erected in our minds have taken many years to tear down and replace with new habits of thinking based on God's Word.

In my own life, as an adult child of an alcoholic, I had some real issues buried in the depths of my personality. The first was a poor self-image and a victim consciousness. I was being victimized by the disruption of my childhood environment because of alcoholism.

Add to this the fact that I was raised in a totally non-Christian environment and taught that Christians were anti-sex, anti-love, and anti-joy. My household environment was adversely influenced by a humanistic philosophy which held that those who believed in the Bible were primitive, superstitious people who needed to invent a God in order to explain away life's mysteries. No one in my family had any conception of the actual power of God to change lives.

Through the study of the promises in God's Word, I discovered there was a reason to be optimistic about my life and a reason for living. Additionally, I moved from a fear-based consciousness to a faith-based one. I discovered there was a supernatural power from a real God who would work on my behalf if I trusted in Him. This gave me the tremendous inner confidence and belief necessary to try to achieve things I never thought possible.

Although I have experienced many adverse circumstances in my life, I have learned to operate on kingdom principles. Since I began to do so, I have known peace of mind. I've also been blessed with a happy and fulfilling marriage with wonderful children. In my career, I have written a number of books, produced feature films, and spoken at various places across the nation. None of this would have been possible apart from Jesus Christ.

Once I turned my life over to Christ and began walking with Him, it was as if I suddenly had "good luck" and many wonderful things began to happen. But it wasn't good luck. It was God's blessing upon my life that brought these good things my way. I do not want to paint an unrealistic picture of walking with Christ. There have been many struggles and long-term challenges and not everything has gone the way I would have liked for it to go. But if you look at the big picture of my life, it is truly blessed and wonderful because of God's goodness.

22

IDENTITY: A PERSONAL QUEST TO FIND SELF-ESTEEM

Since my earliest childhood years, I wanted to know the answer to the questions: *Who am I? What is my purpose in life?* and *Why am I here?* As a very young boy, I was intensely curious about these key questions in life, and I remember that neither my parents nor the educational system to which I was exposed ever spoke about these matters. I found that very, very strange!

In my youth, I wanted who I was. The subjects I was required to study in school did not give me the answers I wanted. It was very hard for me to concentrate on mundane school subjects while these questions burned inside me. I began to study on my own as early as in the third grade. With books from the library I read biographies of great scientists and inventors, hoping they could supply me with the answers I was searching for. I studied the lives of Albert Einstein, Nicola Tesla, Madam Curie, Thomas Edison, Enrico Fermi, Louis Pasteur and on and on. Later, I also read about nuclear physics, biology, and other sciences. I soon discovered, however, that modern science did not have the answers to life's most important questions.

I began studying psychology by reading the books of Sigmund Freud, Carl Jung, Fritz Perls and I studied such subjects as reality therapy, psychoanalysis, and Gestalt therapy. Here, too, I could not find what I was looking for. Then, when the counterculture exploded and men like Harvard professor Dr. Timothy Leary advocated the use of psychedelic drugs, I went in that direction. I read books such as *Heaven and Hell* and *The Doors of Perception* by Aldous Huxley. The talk was about leaving this reality for another by traveling through the doors of perception by using psychedelic drugs.

It was then, while still in my teens, that I began experimenting with not only mescaline, but LSD and peyote mushrooms. These mind-blowing experiences paved the way for my investigations into Eastern mysticism. I began practicing Zen Buddhism, Hinduism, yoga, meditation, astral projection, and followed the teachings of the guru Baba Ram Dass and a whole host of other Eastern mystical teachers.

Before I finished, I did research on Scientology, est, Carlos Casteneda, Stephen Gaskin, Jane Roberts, Edgar Cayce, and many other "spiritual teachers." I was also dropping acid and majoring in the new college accredited field of Altered States of Consciousness at the University of Missouri, where we studied related subjects scientifically.

The purpose of this spiritual pilgrimage was simply to find the answers to the life questions I posed at the beginning of this chapter: *Who am I? What is my purpose in life? Why am I here?*

It was not until I encountered members of the Jesus Movement who challenged me to read the books of men such as Dr. Francis Schaeffer, the great philosopher and theologian, that I began to come up with answers.

After reading Dr. Schaeffer, I was shocked to find that Christians could be intelligent and that there was a logical, and airtight, intellectual defense of biblical Christianity.

I attended a "Christian Religious Retreat" outside Columbia, Missouri. Unfortunately, I was completely turned off by this religious gathering because nobody had any answers. I hitchhiked back to the campus, receiving one ride from a Pentecostal preacher and his wife and another from a Bible salesman with a station wagon full of Bibles. Both of the men shared the Gospel of Jesus Christ with me and I ended up inviting Him into my life on the back roads of Missouri. It was then that I knew I had found God for the first time--not the illusory or mystical experiences my adventures in the New Age had given me. I knew I had found the real thing. I also found the answers to my three questions. *I knew instantly that I was a child of God and here on Earth for a reason.* •

You cannot find your identity until you find your Creator. Not one of us is here by accident. Each of us is here for a reason. Life is not meaningless! Each of us has an identity because we are created by God. It is possible to know our identity once we know God.

This is the foundational truth in experiencing breakthrough in our lives—that of knowing who we are. The good news is that God has made it possible for each of us to know who we are when we know Jesus Christ. All we have to do is *ask!*

23

THE PRINCIPLE OF IDENTITY: HEALING YOUR SELF-IMAGE

The Principle of Identity is the core principle in life. If you do not know who you are—and millions of people on this planet do not have the foggiest idea as to their identity—then how can you become who you are supposed to become?

Developing self-esteem and a positive self-image is something that all of us need. Both are rooted in a groundswell of the truth that each of us is created in the image of the personal God of the universe. Subtract Him from the self-esteem equation and you are left with nothing. Life without God is always meaningless.

Yet the Bible declares that we who are in Christ have a true purpose and identity that transcends what our job title is or how expensive our home is. The Apostle Paul states in Ephesians 1:18-23:

> I pray that the eyes of your heart may be enlightened, so that you may know what is the hope of

His calling, what are the riches of the glory of His inheritance in the saints, and what is the surpassing greatness of His power toward us who believe. These are in accordance with the working of the strength of His might which He brought about in Christ, when He raised Him from the dead, and seated Him at His right hand in the heavenly places, far above all rule and authority and power and dominion, and every name that is named, not only in this age, but also in the one to come. And He put all things in subjection under His feet, and gave Him as head over all things to the church, which is His body, the fullness of Him who fills all in all.

People who have accepted Jesus Christ are now in Christ and therefore have a new identity. No matter our station in life, we are actually saints of God. The true biblical definition of the word means that people who have received Jesus Christ are now saints. It means someone who has been filled with the Spirit of God and has become a citizen of an eternal world called the kingdom of heaven.

A true understanding of what the Bible—or a literal revelation of the Word of God—is actually saying would set you free in your inner self. You are not who you have been taught to be! In a sense you have now become as a time traveler or astronaut who, having crash-landed on a remote planet, is living temporarily with the people of that world. So, you who are a saint or citizen of the kingdom of heaven are now connected to a different world even though, at the moment, you are still living on Earth.

Integral to the *Principle of Identity* is that you are an eternal being who, in reality, has been given a tremendous inheritance and power by a Divine King. True, you are now in Earth School for a while. But even though this life has importance and significance, your real home is in heaven. Thus, when you live, eat, and breathe here on planet Earth, you must remember that the body you now live in is only borrowed. It is simply an earth suit you must walk around in for a while.

Clearly, this kind of language can sound other worldly and mystical. The point is that your earthly life is very important, and what you do matters a great deal. You are part of a greater reality than the one your eyes can see, and that is the reality of God's kingdom. It is here that the principles of breakthrough can really be understood. When we learn to harness the power and force of this invisible kingdom into our nitty-gritty reality, we learn that we are saints of the kingdom of heaven and we can release kingdom power into this present physical universe.

This is a very powerful concept. As saints of God, we can tap into power in the invisible realm which can affect our present reality. As people who are in Christ, we can now have the authority that Christ gave us to exercise dominion on the planet. This is what sainthood is about. Being a saint means that we are joint-heirs with Christ and servant/king/priests who have kingdom power to transform our world.

Therefore, our identities should be found in Christ where we are now part of God's family along with its rights and privileges. These are real kingdom keys by which we can exercise the full authority of the believer.

24

ONE FLEW OVER THE CUCKOO'S NEST

When I was growing up, one of my favorite books was Ken Kesey's *One Flew Over the Cuckoo's Nest*, the story of a man who was sent to a mental hospital where the doctors were crazier than the patients. McMurphy, the hero of the book, challenges the system and shows the world that mental patients aren't as crazy as some people think.

Kesey was making a comment about madness in our society, and how many of our national values and beliefs are false.

I really related to this book during my coming of age. Raised in a home without Christian values, I therefore had no answers during my growth years. I looked upon society with all its hypocrisy and phony values and became rebellious.

I did not know God existed, or that He had a plan for my life, and I made many attempts to escape the madness of society. But God, through His love for me, put people into my life to tell me about Jesus Christ. After a great deal of resistance, I finally accepted Christ and found the answers I had so long sought.

I became a person under construction by the Holy Spirit. Layer after layer of pain and sadness was removed as God was rebuilding me from the inside. He began to reshape my thought patterns and ideas about who I was and about what life was all about.

I discovered firsthand what a marvelous adventure our lives can become when we let God direct our paths. I understood that He loved me and only wanted me to be everything I had been created to be. He sent His power into my life to make this happen.

God said, "Look at these wonderful dreams I have for you, Paul. They are going to be yours and I am going to give you My power, My resources, and My strength to make it happen."

25

HOW TO KNOW WHO YOU REALLY ARE THROUGH BLESSING

Our earthly identities and self-images are tied into who our parents are and what our ancestors were. But we also need to know who we are in the Lord. There is a direct relationship between knowing who you really are, and blessing. The amazing thing about accepting Jesus Christ into our lives is that we become completely new people in God's family. Our identities are instantly changed and, once we begin to understand who we really are, the results are powerful and profound.

The blessing of God upon an individual or a nation has a direct and powerful effect upon the destiny of each identity involved. For instance, in the Old Testament, when men such as Jacob were blessed by God, it deeply affected their identities. It says in Genesis 35:9-12,

> Then God appeared to Jacob again when he came from Paddan-aram, and He blessed him. And

115

God said to him, "Your name is Jacob; you shall no longer be called Jacob, but Israel shall be your name." Thus He called him Israel. God also said to him, "I am God Almighty; be fruitful and multiply; a nation and a company of nations shall come from you, and kings shall come forth from you. And the land which I gave to Abraham and Isaac, I will give it to you, and I will give the land to your descendants after you."

Here we see the power of God's blessing changing a man's life forever. When God blessed Jacob, his life, his identity, and self-image were radically and profoundly transformed.

Turning to the New Testament, in Galatians 3:14 it says, "In order that in Christ Jesus the blessing of Abraham might come to the Gentiles, so that we might receive the promise of the Spirit through faith." This means that, in Jesus Christ, the blessings of Abraham are ours. This blessing was passed on from generation to generation, and can be found in passages such as Deuteronomy 28:1-14:

Now it shall be, if you will diligently obey the Lord your God, being careful to do all His commandments which I command you today, the Lord your God will set you high above all the nations of the earth.

And all these blessing shall come upon you and overtake you, if you will obey the Lord your God.

Blessed shall you be in the city, blessed shall you be in the country,

Blessed shall be the offspring of your body and the produce of your ground and the offspring of your beasts, the increase of your herd and the young of your flock.

Blessed shall be your basket and your kneading bowl.

Blessed shall you be when you come in, and blessed shall you be when you go out.

The Lord will cause your enemies who rise up against you to be defeated before you; they shall come out against you one way and shall flee before you seven ways.

The Lord will command the blessing upon you in your barns and in all that you put your hand to, and He will bless you in the land which the Lord your God gives you.

The Lord will establish you as a holy people to Himself, as He swore to you, if you will keep the commandments of the Lord your God, and walk in His ways.

So all the peoples of the earth shall see that you are called by the name of the Lord; and they shall be afraid of you.

And the Lord will make you abound in prosperity, in the offspring of your body and in the offspring of your beast and in the produce of your ground, in the land which the Lord swore to your fathers to give you.

The Lord will open for you His good storehouse, the heavens, to give rain to your land in its season and to bless all the work of your hand; and you shall lend to many nations, but you shall not borrow.

And the Lord shall make you the head and not the tail, and you only shall be above, and you shall not be underneath, if you will listen to the commandments of the Lord your God, which I charge you today, to observe them carefully, and do not turn aside from any of the words which I command you today, to the right or to the left, to go after other gods to serve them.

Clearly, these blessings should create a profound change in the identity of any Christian believer. Nonetheless, the contemporary believer may have difficulties with these promises of blessing. First, there can be a misinterpretation of what they actually mean. They should not be misconstrued to mean that once people have accepted Jesus Christ, they are never going to experience heartache, disappointment, adversity, persecution, or pain.

When I was speaking at the Sunday evening service at Angelus Temple in Los Angeles, Dr. Harold Helms, the church pastor—and a man committed to work in the inner city—had missionaries from Pakistan introduced who were under intense persecution in their own country. Dr. Helms made the comment that, "If any teaching will not play over there, then it is not true." What he meant was that nowhere does the Bible teach that the Christian will enjoy a life free from trial, persecution, and adversity. The blessing of God does not guarantee you a Beverly Hills mansion, instant riches, or fame. Nor will your life become an effortless, primrose path to heaven.

The Bible *does* promise you blessing in every area of your life as well as God's prosperity for you. All the promises in the Bible are yours, but not automatically. You must receive them by faith, diligently apply kingdom principles to your life, and obey. You must walk in the light of the total Scripture.

These promises should make a powerful change in how you see the world and yourself in it. As a believer in Jesus Christ, you should expect God to move powerfully, dramatically, and miraculously in your life and the lives of those you pray for.

Secondly, people who read the promises in God's Word, as in Deuteronomy 28, may consciously or unconsciously, trivialize or demean their importance. Not only is Christianity truth, but all of God's words are true! Every Christian can rely upon them absolutely. God's promises of powerful and life-changing blessing are true for our lives and our world. They should never be treated as meaningless, outdated, or irrelevant. Either they are true or they are not. The bottom line is that God's promises can be relied upon in every circumstance of a Christian's life.

When we read Deuteronomy 28, we should not minimize the incredible power of God's Word. Sadly, there are many who do so. But no Christian should follow their example. When Moses came down with the commandments on the tablets of stone, he found that the Israelites had lost their faith and reverted to idolatry. But just because the Israelites were unfaithful in this instance

did not make God's existence doubtful or His commandments unworthy of obedience.

The critical point here is that either all of the Bible is
true truth or it is not. The account of Adam and Eve,
Noah and the flood, and Christ's resurrection are not
merely Sunday school stories without relevance to our
world. God's Word is true, not because we have conned
ourselves into believing it or have whipped ourselves
into an emotional frenzy. It is true because it is true. As
Dr. Francis Schaeffer said, it is a final reality.

So when we read Deuteronomy 28, or the account of
Christ's resurrection, we must allow the truth of these
accounts to totally transform our lives. Our identity thus
becomes changed and, once our identity is transformed,
we acquire the ability to live in the world as believing,
effective Christians. Therefore Deuteronomy 28 should
lead us to expect that God will move in our lives positively and profoundly, affecting our resources, our relationships, our business, our children, our society, and our
world.

Just think of the changes that would have happened
in inner-city Los Angeles if the youth had been taught
that they were here for a reason and that they could have
expected God's blessing in their lives. The hopelessness,
despair, and bitterness would have been driven out by
a greater truth. The riots, lootings, and burnings would
not have happened.

This is not to say the effects of racism, poverty, and
lack of education would have been solved by some wav-
ing of a religious magic wand. But once the core of a
person's identity has been positively affected by the truth

of God's Word, there are far-reaching effects. People begin to live as they see themselves, and people of faith and
hope can achieve far greater things than people who
have neither faith nor hope.

When we believe and expect God's goodness, then we
let God become a partner in our lives. Kingdom resources also become ours, and we can expect to see the power of those resources in our lives.

26

THE PRINCIPLE OF THE FINAL INTEGRATION POINT

FINDING PERSONAL WHOLENESS

Dr. Francis Schaeffer, world-renowned philosopher and theologian, coined the phrase "the final integration point." Basically, his term means that each person seeks a means by which to bring their whole lives together.

Through all the centuries, man has sought different methods and ways to give his life meaning. Some try to give meaning to their lives by earning money or through their careers. For others the choice may be romantic love, sex, art, sports, family, fishing, gaining power, or religion. Careers, art, and the pursuit of pleasure have become common, final integration points in our time.

People who limit their pursuits to these things usually began to unravel at some point, because such pursuits are not capable of giving life meaning. The woman who puts all her hopes into marrying the right guy, the man who struggles to reach the top of his profession, writers who throw themselves into their work in quest for meaning—all end up bitterly disillusioned.

Only God can become a person's final integration point. Any attempt to integrate one's life apart from Jesus Christ is destined for disaster. *The Principle of the Final Integration Point* is profound, but simple. If you violate it, even as a Christian, you are going to walk down empty roads. I know of many Christians who love Christ but, knowingly or not, do not live by this principle. If they were honest, they would acknowledge their real final integration point is not Jesus Christ but their pursuits of acting, money-making, careers, writing, and even the ministry and religious work.

I considered my filmmaking career as my final integration point. For many years, my wife Kristina's final integration point was her acting. When anything besides God is your final integration point, it tends to become idolatrous.

To really experience breakthrough, we must put God first and allow Christ to be our final integration point. We must allow our relationship with Christ to come before work, ministry, or other pursuits. We must really listen to Him, allowing Him to establish our priorities, and partner with Him through life.

There is immense spiritual and psychological freedom in having Christ integrate your life. You are certain of your identity and you know what God wants you to do with your life. The key to discovering the power of *The Principle of the Final Integration Point* is not necessarily to go off to some foreign country as a missionary, even though that may be what God wants you to do. The key is to live your life in the fullness of God, a life of worship to Christ.

27

THE POWER OF MORAL PURITY
IN YOUR LIFE

The Principle of the Power of Moral Purity is a key to successful living. It is a foundational principle. There are always bad consequences if this principle is violated. Yielding to sin always brings a loss of power into an individual's life.

We live in a culture which still teaches "if it feels good, do it," despite the undeniable realities of incurable or fatal social diseases or the destructiveness of alcoholism and drug addiction. Basketball superstar Magic Johnson's tragedy illustrates society's loss of understanding of the power of sin to deprive individuals of power. Magic Johnson's tremendous career in professional basketball was cut short because he contracted the HIV virus. He would still be playing basketball today if he had governed his behavior appropriately.

God is not sitting up in heaven looking for ways to ruin people's fun. God created us as men and women,

125

and that means that He also created us as sexual beings with sexual needs and desires that require fulfillment. Yet people think that God is somehow anti-sex. He is not. God created sex to be richly enjoyed by a married woman and man in the liberating context of a faithful and pure relationship. He restricted sexual expression to the boundaries of marriage because it was part of His design for the power of sex to be creative within marriage, but destructive outside of it.

This is a specific illustration of how following the commandments of God actually results in the possibility of real power and creativity. Conversely, deciding to ignore God's law in favor of a sinful course of action always leads to a loss of power in the individual.

The way it works, once you accept Jesus Christ, is that God actually lives inside you in the Person of the Holy Spirit. You reach a place where you are filled, or baptized, with His Spirit. You are filled with power from on high. Once the Holy Spirit is within, a living energy burns there, expressing a form of power that is available to you. When the Person of the Holy Spirit lives within and controls your personality, you become a powerful person radiating purpose, peace, creativity, and joy. Such good things as love, peace, patience, kindness, and self-control are the positive results.

It says in Galatians 5:22-23: "...but the fruit of the Spirit is love, joy, peace, patience, kindness, goodness, faithfulness, gentleness, self-control...." This means that God's power within you produces these qualities. But, if you short-circuit the power of God through sin and disobedience, then the power that God gives to the faithful believer is no longer available to you, and you begin to live on limited human power. Living on purely human energy, or the flesh, results in the following:

> Now the deeds of the flesh are evident, which are: immorality, impurity, sensuality, idolatry, sorcery, enmities, strife, jealousy, outbursts of anger, disputes, dissensions, factions, envying, drunkenness, carousing, and things like these, of which I forewarn you just as I have forewarned you that those who practice such things shall not inherit the kingdom of God.
>
> (Galatians 5:19-21)

When you sin and disobey God, you distance yourself from your source of power, because God is not simply talking about living in the heaven of the future. He is talking about living the power of the kingdom of heaven right now where you are. The Bible says when you are in the power of the Spirit, you will have self-control, or the power to manage your life. When you are cut off from God's power, you lose this ability and lose the divine source of that self-control.

Many Christians today have completely missed the point about not sinning and living in the power of God. These Christians say, in effect, "I better not sin because God wants me to be good." But, at the same time, they secretly want to sin—and end up doing so—because this point of view, while it holds *some* truth (after all, God *does* want us to be good people), doesn't go far enough.

God does want you to be free of sin, but that's not all He wants. He has already said, "It is impossible to be good apart from faith in Christ!" Trusting Christ is the only way to earn favor with God. His desire that you do not sin is so that you can be powerful and become all you were created to be. God knows that sin cuts you off from your source of power, which is himself.

The Principle of the Power of Moral Purity means that God's power flows through you when you are pure. Sin disconnects you from the power source, and it is precisely here that the devil works his deception. People think the issue is sex, drug abuse, or other sins, but that is not true. The devil is interested in cutting you off from God because he wants to destroy you. It's the Garden of Eden all over again. The devil promised Adam and Eve that they would be like gods. But the promise proved false and Adam and Eve were cast out of the Garden of Eden. The devil's intentions have not changed throughout history: promise everything and give nothing.

STRONGHOLDS OF BONDAGE IN YOUR MIND

One area of bondage in the human personality is sexuality. Sex is such a powerful, God-given creative force, but ideas about sexuality are often distorted or perverted in our fallen world. On a deeply subconscious level, ideas, beliefs, and thought patterns regarding sex or eroticism might easily become perverted through the constant bombardment of false images and the spirit of lust preying upon our personalities.

God is not against sex. He created men and women to be sexual creatures, capable of enjoying the beauties and intimacies of a sexual relationship. His perfect plan is for the sexual relationship to find its widest and most complete fulfillment within marriage.

Another element that must be introduced into this area is Satan, a deceiver and perverter of all of God's creations. The devil wants to pervert sex so that it becomes something sick and twisted rather than an expression of love. His game plan for the human race is intended to pervert our sexuality with pornography, sadomasochism, homosexuality, rape, child abuse, and other such satanic devices.

By creating strongholds of perversion and lust in the human soul, and by linking these perversions to sexual satisfaction, the devil creates in our fallen human natures inner patterns that link such perversions with emotional satisfaction.

The advertising industry has done this for years by linking smoking a cigarette to being handsome, pretty, or successful. Actually, the idea of smoking and being intelligent or attractive have absolutely nothing to do with each other. But, exposing someone to repeated images which suggest that lighting up a particular brand of cigarette is linked to being attractive or "having it together" will result in the human mind becoming brainwashed, and a subconscious association is made.

The devil's strategy is to create bondage in our personalities so that sin can interrupt the flow of God's Spirit through us. God wants us to experience breakthrough and deliverance in this area. He doesn't want His children having bondages or self-destructive strongholds.

Remember, a stronghold is always based on deception. When God's Word comes into our beings and shines light upon us, deliverance occurs. No longer must you believe the lie that sinful thinking has a payoff. Real sexual happiness is to be found in obeying God's Word, allowing our sexual responses to flower under the Lordship of Christ.

Sexual immorality—in thought or deed—produces emotional slavery. A person whose mind is captured by such strongholds is not free to enjoy sex. The Bible says, "Or do you not know that the unrighteous shall not inherit the kingdom of God? Do not be deceived; neither fornicators, nor idolaters, nor effeminate, nor homosexuals ... shall inherit the kingdom of God."

The maximum expression of life and human sexuality can only be found within the liberating laws of love. Only within these laws can the Christian find true freedom.

28

HOW TO CHANGE
YOUR THINKING ABOUT SEX

PRACTICAL STEPS TO SEXUAL PURITY

The following steps can be taken to destroy strongholds in the human mind which embody false beliefs about sex:

Step One: Believe God's plan. Allow the Holy Spirit and the Word of God to govern your actions.

Step Two: Surrender your mind to the Lordship of Christ and think only those thoughts which represent God's view of sex.

Step Three: Renounce a spirit of lust. Do not allow yourself to be deceived by media images which have nothing to do with the kind of life a Christian should lead.

Step Four: Ask the Holy Spirit to purify you and aid you in your quest for sexual purity. Trust the Holy Spirit to create wholesome new thought patterns about sex.

Step Five: Talk to God about everything that goes on in your mind and heart. Do not let the enemy condemn you. Allow yourself to be cleansed by the blood of Christ and healed.

Step Six: Read and listen to the Word of God and allow it to be absorbed into your inner being.

Step Seven: Trust God's goodness that He will lead you and guide you. Obey Him and step out on faith.

DISCOVER THE WONDERFUL YOU

People everywhere are trying to find themselves. I understand this quest for self-understanding, because I devoted the earlier part of my life attempting to answer the questions: *Who am I? What is my purpose in life? Why am I here?*

I didn't find the answers to those questions until I entered into a personal relationship with Jesus Christ. There was something profoundly different about Jesus Christ. My involvement with Eastern mysticism and illicit drugs had resulted in emotional highs, but they seemed illusory and false. But when I found Jesus Christ I knew that, even on an experiential level, I had found the real thing.

What impressed me most about the God of the Bible was that He was the God of the universe was a distinct person. What a tremendous contrast to mystical teachings that God was only an energy force, some kind of higher consciousness. The true God has a personality, and He has also created us to have distinct personalities.

The truth of that should absolutely astound you! He knows you by name and He knows everything about you and still loves you. Each of us was created as a unique individual and personality. God designed each unique personality and it is sacred. The Bible tells us that, in truth, we have been created by a personal God as a unique and special people with a place and home in this universe.

This powerful truth about our uniqueness before God has been driven home to me many different ways, but none more powerfully than through the birth of my first child, Paul Christopher McGuire.

After a decade of marriage, we thought perhaps the biological window of opportunity to have a child might be gone. Yet we prayed and had people pray for us. Delores Hayford, the mother of Rev. Jack Hayford, prayed for Kristina after the Gideon Principle Women's Intercessory Prayer meeting that gathered on Tuesdays in the prayer chapel at The Church On The Way. She believed God would give us a child and even wrote the date she prayed for us with her finger over our hearts prophetically. She told us to remember the date because God was going to answer our prayer. God did answer our prayer and Kristina became pregnant.

After a couple of months into Kristina's pregnancy, we went to get an ultrasound test. We do not believe in abortion, but they wanted to look at the baby. There on the ultrasound screen I saw a tiny baby with hands that seemed to wave at me. The personal, living God of the universe is involved in our destinies even from the moment of conception. It was no accident that we had a baby boy.

When baby Paul was born and I saw his little blue eyes and tiny face, it was so powerfully obvious to me that God's hand was in our lives from conception to birth. In Isaiah 44:2 it says, "Thus says the Lord who made you and formed you from the womb, who will help you...." God knew each of us in the womb and is our personal friend.

Gradually, baby Paul became a little person with feelings who smiled, waved, crawled on the floor, and whose eyes sparkled with delight when he saw his parents. When I look at my son, it is so obvious to me that God is the author of life. That little Paul looks and acts like a blend of his parents and grandparents, yet has his own unique personality, is literally as if the heavens shout that God is on the throne of the universe and that He creates life.

All of us are God's special creations and none of us are here by accident. We are people with personalities that are gifts from God. All of the personality traits of every individual human being are the direct results of God's handiwork.

That is why Christianity is truth and other spiritual beliefs are false. The Bible teaches us that we are special to God and that our lives have meaning. Once we understand this, it becomes possible to live a complete and full life. God provides a real foundation for our lives—the truth of His existence and our importance to Him. When we grasp all the implications of that truth, then we are really free.

29

THE PERSONAL LIVING GOD
OF THE UNIVERSE

HOW YOUR HEAVENLY FATHER LOVES YOU

Many people today do not know what it is like to have a real father. Either they come from a single parent home, or the father is often absent from the home on business. Therefore many people do not know what it is like to have a loving father who is concerned with their welfare. The concept of God the Father is not one that has a whole lot of meaning for many people. Perhaps this is why feminists in our nation rebel from the concept of God as a Father or a patriarchal figure. But the reality of God as our Heavenly Father goes even deeper than that. Our entire culture has lost touch with the reality of a personal, living God.

During my spiritual pilgrimage into the New Age and Eastern mysticism, God was neither a Heavenly Father nor even a real person to me. The "God" of the New Age and Eastern religions is a mystical one, defined as a kind of energy force or higher consciousness. This New Age "God" is really just energy or consciousness of which we are all supposedly a part. According to this concept, we are simply the dream of God.

When I was hitchhiking on the backroads of Missouri and invited Jesus Christ into my life, I had an overwhelming encounter with Him. I literally entered into a personal relationship totally unlike anything else I had experienced before. When I accepted Jesus Christ, I saw God for the first time, not in a physical but a spiritual sense. I had found the real thing. All the blissful and higher states of consciousness I had experienced while being involved in Eastern mysticism seemed illusory and unreal when contrasted with meeting Christ.

What struck me as most remarkable is that the real God is not an impersonal energy force. God is personal! He knows us as individuals and special people. That is such an incredible fact. God wants to have a personal relationship with each of us.

We are not here on planet Earth by accident. Each one of us was created by a personal God who knows us by name. Really grasping that fact can completely revolutionize our existence. It can be intensely liberating to understand that we are here for a reason and a purpose and that we have a Heavenly Father who loves us individually.

A real and caring God is intimately involved with us and is helping us. Our lives should be a celebration of this fact. This is what produces true evangelism and wins people to Christ. When we celebrate in our hearts the reality of God's existence and goodness, the flow of the miraculous begins to happen.

BACK IN THE SANDBOX

One of the most powerful breakthrough principles I have ever discovered is *The Principle of Playfulness.* Jesus Christ taught this principle when He said, "Unless you become like little children, you shall never enter the kingdom of heaven." Artists understand this principle, but unfortunately many religious people do not. True Christianity was never supposed to become the list of dos and don'ts, or the dead orthodoxy, it has so often become. Christianity is supposed to be a celebration of life.

I have learned more about God the Father and Christianity by crawling around on the floor chasing my one-year-old than anywhere else. As I get belly-down on the kitchen floor and play with the pots and pans, I begin to see the world through the fresh eyes of a little child again. It is as if I am seeing everything for the very first time. When I crawl through the grass in the park with my son as he discovers interesting bugs and gentle breezes for the first time, I am there with him rediscovering God's world and the universe all over again and remembering things I had forgotten long ago.

Spirituality is not about dry bones! It is about the river of life and wading and splashing around deep in it. When I bathe my kid and watch him giggle as he sloshes around in the bathtub, I learn about the river of living water God has for us.

It is my frank opinion that some of the preachers and evangelists of today need to go down to local parks and crawl through the grass with little kids. Some of these Christian therapists need to take the day off and go with their patients to a grassy park on a summer's day and laugh together with them. I know I needed that. There is something profoundly spiritual about chasing bugs in the grass with a little child who can only gurgle and not talk.

Breakthrough in our lives just seems to happen when we celebrate God's goodness and abandon our cares. Maybe the best thing for all of us is to get our shovels and pails and get in the sandbox with Jesus. I have a sneaking hunch that if we learned how to be like little children again, we could transform our world for Christ!

30

UNDERSTANDING THE GENERATIONAL CURSE IN YOUR FAMILY

Who you are today is a composite of the choices you have made, your experiences, and the mental, spiritual, and emotional environment in which you were raised.

A prime example of this would be when Adam and Eve disobeyed God in the Garden of Eden and allowed sin to enter the world. We read in First Corinthians 15:22, "For as in Adam all die, so also in Christ all shall be made alive" (NAS). Adam and Eve not only passed on their physical characteristics to their descendants, but, because of their disobedience, they are also responsible for sin and death.

So, too, our parents pass along to us both physical and spiritual characteristics. Such things as alcoholism, sex problems, the occult, depression, and other spiritual forces move from one generation to another until they are broken by the power of God's Word. These things are not simply psychological problems that are modeled in dysfunctional homes, although this too may be a powerful contributing factor.

RE-ENACTMENT

When asked, "Why is there so much abuse in families and violence in society?", family expert John Bradshaw pointed out that deep psychological problems are passed on from one generation to another through "re-enactment."

> A great deal of what we call normal child-parenting is being carried down multi-generationally from parent to parent.
>
> *John Bradshaw*

This is the term used to describe people acting out on others the same things that happened to them as children, whether good happenings or bad. As an example, victims of child abuse often become child abusers themselves. Statistics say that between forty to fifty percent of child molesters were abused as children, and they re-enact this abuse upon other children as a means of dealing with their own inner shame and powerlessness.

A classic example in modern history is Adolf Hitler. Bradshaw theorizes that he was able to seduce Germany—a highly-civilized and educated nation—because the German family unit was in trouble. At that time Germany's family unit was structured on a strict autocratic format with the father literally the dictator of the family system. Psychologists theorize there was a great deal of repressed rage in German society. Bradshaw comments,

"Hitler was a gang leader for a bunch of adolescents acting out the rage they were subjected to as children."

In her book, *For Your Own Good*, Alice Miller characterizes Hitler's childhood as abusive. He was supposedly beaten daily by his father, who himself may have been of Jewish ancestry.

Christians mistakenly super-spiritualize life and history by saying that Adolf Hitler was satanically possessed. He may well have been, or at least used by evil. But there are very real psychological circumstances leading up to this yielding to satanic forces. Evil takes advantage of negative human experiences to gain footholds in—and thereby control of—peoples' lives. It is true that evil is personal and can operate supernaturally. However, evil is allowed entrance through such very human, negative emotions as hatred, abuse, bitterness, rejection, and violence.

Therefore, a pattern of re-enactment can be seen taking place when we look at Adolf Hitler and see him unleash the same violence that victimized him as a child. His hatred of Jews cannot be dismissed by regarding it as a manifestation of Satan's hatred for God's chosen people. True as that may be, Hitler's hatred for the Jews may also have been caused by his rage against his father's violence. Satan uses very real events to cause death and destruction.

The family unit's historical importance is why the powers of darkness have long sought to destroy it. Such destruction of a healthy family can provide the psychological and spiritual weaknesses to unleash greater evil upon the human race. As biblical Christians we must recognize that we have an adversary who exploits real human weaknesses.

Studies show that many murderers and rapists often re-enact the violence that was done to them as children. In case after case of violent criminals, we see that "people who live with violence become violent." Children who are beaten become abusers. Children who join the dangerous, violent gangs in our inner cities are invariably the direct products of broken family units and isolation by society.

It has been said that black families were able to provide leadership in times of slavery to hold the family units together. While white families have hardly been exempt, it is true that in more recent times the black family, as an institution, has lacked its traditional strength in dealing with the pressures of modern life. Thus, violence in the inner cities is erupting, precisely as a direct consequence of family-unit breakdown. It is not a unique problem of black families. This is creating major problems in white communities today, as well. Thus we see drug addiction, alcoholism, and Satanism on the increase.

BREAKING THE GENERATIONAL CURSE IN YOUR FAMILY—
SPECIFIC THINGS YOU CAN DO

How do you break the generational curse? To accomplish anything you must have clear cut goals and objectives. To do nothing means only that you will continue to have all the problems and difficulties that you have now. The first thing to do is to identify specific behaviors you want to change and write them down. Some of these behaviors could be the following:

(1) Poverty consciousness and failure mind set.
(2) Fear addiction.
(3) Poor self-image.
(4) Poor communication skills in marriage.
(5) Victim consciousness.

You may be able to identify other damaging behaviors, but the basic principle, of course, remains the same. What is important is to recognize the negative behavior and write it down.

Remember, the negative behaviors you have identified cause you to act in damaging ways. Though there may be the temptation to do nothing, it is important at this point to remember two things: no matter what the circumstances of your life were, you are responsible for your present and future behavior. And you are not helpless; you have been given the power to change.

This power to change will involve forming new patterns of behavior for yourself. Dealing with any of the five problems mentioned above entails changing those negative patterns for positive ones. It will help you to change if you make a list of any of these positive patterns you wish to develop.

The following could be a list of newer, positive characteristics:

(1) Success consciousness and winning mind set.
(2) Fear turned into faith equals power.
(3) Positive self-image.
(4) Good communication skills in marriage.
(5) Non-victim or leader consciousness.

None of these new characteristics will automatically replace the old ones, But if we have them as goals, we can decide what we need to do to achieve them. We will have to retrain our minds with new habits of thinking and perception. God has given us that freedom and responsibility; it is God who gives us the divine privilege of redesigning our lives under His guidance.

We must teach ourselves to think and act in the manner in which we want to become. Perhaps we do not know how to do these things. Then we will have to do some homework and research to find out how other people with these attributes live, behave, act, and use them as role models to duplicate these behaviors. And even though we pray with confidence for His help, strength, and guidance, God expects us to be active participants in our own growth program. Jesus Christ tells us we can be whole, but we are going to have to have faith and work at it.

Recently, we have begun to remodel our home. My wife had a vision of what she wanted the home to look like. She shared that vision with me and together we worked to redesign and rebuild it into that desired image. In a sense our home was like a dysfunctional family—it did not provide the living environment we wanted.

So we hired plumbers, carpenters, and tile men to rip out and replace old fixtures with new ones to our liking. We also got rid of the old furniture and replaced it with new. Slowly, our home began to conform with our new vision and expectations. The remodeling is not yet complete, but we are happy with the way things are turning out.

God has bestowed upon us that same creative power to improve our lives, to redesign them, and change the way we live. We no longer have to be victims of our circumstances. But we are going to have to do some hard work, quite a bit of praying, and lots of remodeling.

31

HOW TO BREAK THE GENERATIONAL CURSE OF WORRY

Sometimes we find ourselves beset with fear and anxiety, overwhelmed with problems and concerns. Financial worries, health fears, concerns over children—the parade of fears and anxieties can go on and on. We developed a *Habit of Fear* and this habit is often passed from generation to generation.

As children, we watched how our parents handled life's challenges. Did they give in to anxieties and fears? Were they worried all the time? Did they respond to life's challenges in inadequate ways? Unconsciously, we began to model their behavior patterns and became conditioned to deal with problems the same way. Even after accepting Christ, the mechanics of these worry habits do not just disappear. They must be actively dismantled by the power of the Holy Spirit. Our minds must be renewed by the Word of God.

The first step in freeing ourselves from the *Habit of Fear* is to recognize that we have developed it. Our enemy in the invisible realm knows this and actively works to cause us fear and worry. The adversary does this to destroy our relationship with God, damage our health, rob us of joy, produce strife, cause divorce, and set us up for drug, alcohol, and other addictions to try to escape the inner torment these fears can bring.

To find release from this reinforced fear-worry habit, we must acknowledge it to as sin and ask to be forgiven and healed. Then we must replace the fear-worry mechanism with a new one, which is *The Rejoice-Trust Habit.* In Philippians 4:4-7, we see a plan for our personal deliverance:

> Rejoice in the Lord always—delight, gladden yourselves in Him, again I say, Rejoice! Let all men know and perceive and recognize your unselfishness—your considerateness, your forbearing spirit. The Lord is near—He is coming soon. Do not fret or have anxiety about anything, but in every circumstance and in everything by prayer and petition (definite requests) with thanksgiving continue to make your wants known to God. And God's peace (be yours, that tranquil state of a soul assured of its salvation through Christ, and so fearing nothing from God and content with its earthly lot of whatever sort that is, that peace) which transcends all understanding, shall garrison and mount guard over your hearts and minds in Christ Jesus.
>
> (Amplified)

Here we see a step-by-step plan for finding freedom from worry and fear and discovering peace of mind. First, we "must rejoice in the Lord always!" We do not rejoice in the Lord just because we feel like it, but as a choice and a decision of our will. The feelings will follow.

In other words, we don't wake up in the morning and give in to the Monday, Tuesday, or any other-day blues. We shake off depressing feelings and anxieties—not giving in but ignoring them! We choose to rejoice in the Lord in whatever circumstance we find ourselves. We walk in an attitude of praise and worship no matter how we feel.

Next, we stop the fear-worry habit by not fearing and worrying. "Do not fret or have anxiety about anything." Through the power of the Holy Spirit, we can stop yielding to a spirit of fear! It may not happen without a fight, but we can break this fear-worry habit and replace it with prayer, trust, and thanksgiving. This way we cast our cares upon the Lord and pray and trust Him to move on our behalf. Thus we walk before the Lord, trusting Him for everything.

The result is that we will walk in the tranquility of peace from God—a powerful peace that will actually guard our hearts and minds. The tranquility of soul which comes from walking with the Lord is a deeper dimension of trust. A fresh sense of joy will spring up from within, overflowing with the peace and power that God has released into our lives. And there will be secondary benefits of increases in energy, creativity, intelligence, harmony in relationships, better dreams, and an improved quality of life. Though we are responsible for making ourselves available to receive them, God is always ready and willing to make these good things available to us.

32

HOW TO BREAK THE CURSE OF FEAR

The generational curse of fear began in the Garden of Eden immediately after Adam and Even disobeyed God and ate of the forbidden fruit. In Genesis 3:9-10, we read, "Then the Lord God called to the man, and said to him, 'Where are you?' And he said, 'I heard the sound of Thee in the garden, and I was afraid because I was naked; so I hid myself.'"

Of the two things to be learned here, the first is that Adam was afraid of God and the second is that Adam's fear was based on his sin. Prior to the fall, the very concept of fear did not exist. Adam and Eve were naked before the fall, but they lived in such a state of total innocence, they did not know this. Adam and Eve were not naive but simply unconscious of the fact of their nakedness—the same way a child may walk around nude and not be ashamed.

Adam became afraid because he ate of the tree of the knowledge of good and evil. He now was aware of his nakedness and had a knowledge of fear, shame, death, and the sin which separated him from God. Thus the psychological force of fear entered the human race and has thundered its terrible voice throughout the generations ever since.

The psychological manifestations of fear include: fear of other people, fear of the dark, fear of heights, fear of failure, fear of poverty, fear of death, fear of rejection, fear of inadequacy, etc. Fear is a spiritual force and its opposite is faith.

When we have faith in God, He provides a covering for our psychological nakedness and we are not ashamed before Him. As believers, God sees us as sinless and pure through the blood of Jesus Christ.

Through Jesus Christ we now have faith instead of fear—faith in God to cover us from our inadequacies and deliver us from such things as poverty, sickness, and defeat.

Second Timothy 2:7 says: "For God hath not given us the spirit of fear; but of power, and of love and of a sound mind" (KJV). The Holy Spirit never produces weirdness, bizarre behavior, or craziness, but instead produces psychological soundness. Breaking the generational curse involves understanding that fear never comes from God and that He has given us sound minds.

Psychological problems such as anxiety, alcoholism, phobias, impotence, homosexuality, eating disorders, drug addiction, neurosis, and compulsive behaviors such as perfectionism are all rooted in fear. When an adult man or woman is stripped to his or her basic emotional components, you will often see a hurt and terrified child who is simply compensating for childhood's wounds by his or her behavior.

Pride is often a compensation and cover-up for fear. Hence we see a mad rush to buy fashionable clothes with designer labels—as if spending money can do anything to solve root psychological problems!

Fear passes from one generation to the next when children imitate their parents' behavior. When a child sees his parents react to situations in terror, or communicate their various fears, the young one learns to react the same way in similar circumstances. Fears that seem natural in teenage and adult years are invariably the result of childhood conditioning.

Conversely, when a child sees his parents living by truly Christian principles and responding to challenges and crises by prayer and reliance on the promises of God, then that child learns to live by faith and not fear. This is how the generational curse of fear is broken.

33

BREAKING THE CURSE OF FEAR AND NEGATIVITY

Good or bad, we unconsciously model our parents' behavior. Fear and negativity are passed from one generation to another by words, perceptions and outlooks on life. In this manner, poverty and failure are often passed on through successive generations. But once we accept Jesus Christ, we no longer have to remain victims of a fear and negativity consciousness!

Recently a great hue and cry has been raised in certain segments of Christian culture over the terms "Positive Thinking" and "Possibility Thinking," as if these concepts were inherently evil. Both can help you live a better life as long as it is clearly understood that salvation does not come from positive or possibility thinking, but through faith in Christ.

Put simply, positive thinking is good for us as long as it is done within a biblical framework and does not become an idol. Positive thinking turned into mind power can be an occult practice, which is dangerous.

No system of thought or teaching—whether positive thinking, faith teaching, or whatever—should separate us from a daily relationship with Jesus Christ.

We must renew our minds with God's Word and think in a disciplined manner in accordance with scriptural promises. We must learn to be aware of our thoughts and let the power of the Holy Spirit take control of our minds.

Moments before writing this chapter, I was barraged by a stream of negative thoughts which tired, depressed, and discouraged me. Then I heard the Holy Spirit say to me, "You are depressed and tired because you are letting negative thinking flow through your mind. You must take charge and redirect your thinking in accordance with My Word." After a moment of quiet revelation, it flashed to me that the enemy was bombarding my mind with a furious assault of negativism. Consciously, deliberately, I began to cease the negative thoughts and reframe my perception based on God's Word. I had to begin trusting God and anchor my hopes on the promises of His Word. At the same time, I had to recognize that life is a spiritual battle, and to be victorious, you must believe and move forward accordingly, trusting in God for the final outcome.

Thus you can break the curse of negativity and fear by choosing to replace it with positive thoughts anchored on the firm reality of who God is and how He works for our good. Many Christians know how to conquer thoughts of lust and hate, yet when it comes to negativity, they let their guard down and the enemy zooms in to shoot them down. Fear and negativity are sins, and if you give into them, they can destroy you.

If you train your mind to see life from the perception of God's Word, you will view challenges positively and release tremendous faith and power into your life to transform it for the better. A positive train of thought in line with God's Word will make you healthy, prosperous, and victorious. A rejuvenating power can pour through you when you practice this principle because your emotions, health, and ability to succeed are all directly tied into your thought habits.

It says in Proverbs: "As a man thinketh in his heart so is he," which means our lives are very much a product of our thoughts. We are to walk with Jesus in a personal manner and this alone should produce positive thoughts, since our Lord lives and moves in the realm of the miraculous.

"All things are possible with God," and we can allow the miracle flow of His power into us through faith in His promises and by thinking as Christ thinks. Our minds must be transformed by the power of His Word for us to become all He created us to be. We are unique and special creations and God desires to unlock all the potential He has placed within us. Cooperation with Jesus Christ allows Him to release us to our full potential. In Christ, we were made to be somebody. By linking up with Christ, we can reach our full, God-given potential which no generational curse or spirit of fear can prevent.

When Jesus Christ is manifest in one's life, there is a tangible, supernatural recharging of the human personality. Nothing less than miracle power energizes us. This supernatural energizing takes place through relationship or communion with God. A life force is released that gives us the power to be healed and live abundantly.

By His grace, God is breathing on these printed words with His Spirit to refresh and infuse you with the sparkling joy of His Spirit. Jesus Christ has the power to set you free if you will receive His word of deliverance. All of heaven's resources will be at your disposal. If the living God was willing to sacrifice His own Son for you, don't you think He has something wonderful in store for you, a reason for you to live?

Despair, depression, and suicidal thoughts must flee as the light of God's kingdom enters your life, bringing with it peace, joy, and happiness. Jesus Christ died to redeem us from the curse of the law so that we might inherit God's blessing. The kingdom of God came into you when you accepted Jesus Christ, making you an heir to a kingdom where there is no poverty, sickness, or sorrow. God has given us the power to defeat the adversary and live as conquerors in this life.

Go into the world as a conqueror, for the "righteous are as bold as a lion." Boldly face life as the overcomer Christ made you to be. Stop trying to identify with the world's image and find your identity in the image of God. Let the image of Christ be formed in you. You are a cosmic adventurer. Act like it. Yours is a royal priesthood in a chosen generation. Behave as such. Remember Daniel, Joseph, Paul, and other men and women of faith. Rise up in newness of life and expect God to do great things. You are a part of the family of God—rejoice in that fact.

34

THE PRINCIPLE OF THANKFULNESS

One of the most liberating principles God has given man in the Bible is *The Principle of Thankfulness.* Personally, it has taken me quite a while to learn this principle.

We read from First Thessalonians 5:18: "In everything give thanks; for this is God's will for you in Christ Jesus." And in Ephesians 5:20 it says, "Always giving thanks for all things in the name of the Lord Jesus Christ to God even the Father." I had read verses like that for years almost unconsciously and without really understanding them. They were just words. But very slowly, God began to show me how powerful this principle really was and He showed me that why I was to give thanks was not for His benefit but mine!

I always assumed the reason we gave thanks to God was because it was the polite thing to do. I thought God enjoyed hearing our appreciation and thanks because it was expected. I didn't understand the life-changing power of being thankful.

Thousands of years ago, God gave the children of Israel the Ten Commandments. One of the Commandments reads, "You shall not covet your neighbor's house; you shall not covet your neighbor's wife or his male servant or his female servant or his ox or his donkey or anything that belongs to your neighbor" (Exod. 20:17, NAS). In other words, don't go around desiring in your heart and being jealous about what everybody else has.

This is covetousness, which is constantly wanting, desiring, and seeking things that are not yours. It implies a restless soul that is always scheming and dreaming about getting material things. Our entire society is built on covetousness and always wanting more than what we have. TV commercials influence us to be dissatisfied unless we have the latest car, home, body, perfume, clothes, shaver, or whatever. Our economy is built on this principle, and we extol the virtues of conspicuous consumption through programs such as *Lifestyles of the Rich and Famous*. What this produces in people—as it did in me — is a lack of thankfulness to God and a constant desire in my heart for "things."

When you are in a state of covetousness, you are not thankful to God. You are in spiritual bondage, a prisoner in a very real sense, because you are unhappy with the way your life is.

I remember walking around Manhattan during my first Christmas after accepting Christ. My heart was bursting with joy and I was thankful to have found the real meaning of Christmas. As I stood near Macy's watching people dashing about madly Christmas shopping, I distinctly recall being filled to overflowing with thanksgiving because I had found Christ and He was so good to me. But this experience slowly dissolved even though I was a committed Christian.

Although I was actually ignorant of the fact that I had a problem in the area of covetousness, the Holy Spirit slowly delivered me from this attitude. It culminated while I was working on my second book in the small bedroom of my cabin-like house nestled in the Hollywood Hills. I was working very hard at a full-time job and writing in my spare time. I looked up at the see-through plastic dome above my head and stopped typing, for suddenly the room was flooded with peace and an overwhelming sense of thanksgiving bubbled in my heart.

I felt the Lord say, "You are exactly where you are supposed to be—in the palm of My hand." It was as if I could see into the invisible realm and know that I was in the center of God's will. I was truly thankful.

These and other experiences led me to understand the power of being thankful and expressing that thanks to God. Living in an attitude of praise and worship to Him sets you free both psychologically and spiritually. Very slowly, I am learning that even in the middle of problems and headaches that God is good and He fills ours lives with many blessings, for which we can be thankful.

God fills us with overflowing blessings, but to enjoy them, we need to learn how to be thankful. In Ecclesiastes 5:19-20, we read: "Furthermore, as for every man to whom God has given riches and wealth, He has also empowered him to eat from them and to receive his reward and rejoice in his labor; this is the gift of God. For he will not often consider the years of his life, because God keeps him occupied with the gladness of his heart."

Being thankful for what you have is a gift from God!

35

HOW TO BREAK THE CURSE OF PERFECTIONISM

Perfectionists very often come from families where they either did not receive enough love and approval, or these were given out only as rewards for performance. Perfectionists often fail to feel accepted or loved by themselves or others; they question their self-worth and worry about other people's opinion of them.

Such people find themselves on an endless treadmill, trying hard to perform well enough to earn the love and acceptance of others. Unfortunately, perfectionists are never able to accomplish this because the root problem is they think they are unlovable and unacceptable no matter what they do!

Nowhere in society is perfectionism more prevalent than in the entertainment industry. Many actors and actresses are motivated to perform well because they perceive this as a means of winning love and acceptance from the general public.

This is a sad state of affairs. God does not want any of His children to exhaust themselves on the treadmill of perfectionism. He does not accept us through performance or deeds, but through the free gift of salvation in Jesus Christ. We can do nothing to earn God's love. He already loves us unconditionally and accepts us fully on the basis of the free gift of salvation. We insult God by trying to earn His love. We are accepted and loved totally by God because of our faith in Christ.

It is one thing to understand truth intellectually and quite another to understand it emotionally. The perfectionist must allow the Spirit of God to come to him and love him on a deep inner level because of Christ.

Since perfectionism is a psychological illness and a sin which harms us, Jesus wants to deliver us from this bondage. Perfectionists not only have trouble loving themselves but loving and accepting others as well. An outward manifestation of the perfectionist's inner self-hatred is the fact that such a person is often very critical of other people. Jesus can heal the perfectionist when he is willing to get off the treadmill and experience God's love. Prayer with a trusted friend or minister is perhaps one way to start to find lasting healing.

By admitting his pain and his feelings of being unloved, the perfectionist can come to Jesus Christ and ask God to heal him. Through prayer and the Holy Spirit, God will let the perfectionist know His unconditional love for him and he will find release from his torment. The inner condemnation can be replaced by the love of Christ and real joy and peace can result. The Holy Spirit will mend your broken past and embrace you to the depths of your being.

If you suffer from perfectionism, I encourage you to go to God and let him hug you as a loving father would his child. When you feel—really feel—His embrace, you may start to weep as God's love for you becomes real. Feel the walls of rejection come tumbling down in your soul as you experience His total love and acceptance for you.

36

HOW TO BREAK THE GENERATIONAL CURSE OF ALCOHOL AND DRUG ABUSE

The curse of alcohol and drug addiction often runs in families and affects many millions of Americans. Children of alcoholics frequently become alcohol or drug addicts themselves. The extent of the problem can also be illustrated by the fact that many centers for treatment of drug and alcohol dependency now exist. Alcoholics Anonymous and Adult Children of Alcoholics (ACOA) chapters have sprung up everywhere.

Janet Geringer Woititz, Ed.D., in her book *Adult Children of Alcoholics* made these observations on alcoholism:

1. Alcoholism runs in families. Rarely do we see cases in isolation. Someone somewhere else in the family usually has been or is currently suffering from the disease.
2. Children of alcoholics run a higher risk of developing alcoholism than children in the main-

stream of the population. There may have been some discussion of environment or genetics, or a combination of both, but the truth of the statement is without question.

3. Children of alcoholics tend to marry alcoholics. They rarely go into a marriage with that knowledge, but we see this phenomenon occur over and over again.

I recognized the generational curse of alcoholism at work in my family a number of years after I became a Christian. Both my wife and I know that alcoholism has run in our families for several generations. I believe I would have become an alcoholic had I not accepted Jesus Christ.

Most alcoholics and drug abusers have good jobs and are often overachievers. Many great actors, business people, movie directors, authors, and military leaders of our day have had, or still have, serious problems with drug or alcohol dependency. These addictions usually result in a storm of other problems. The image of the alcoholic as only a skid row bum is false. Alcoholics come from every walk of life.

For me the spirit of alcoholism was broken when I accepted Jesus Christ as my Lord and Savior and was baptized in the Holy Spirit. It was not instantaneous, but as I began to read the Word of God, pray, and worship God regularly, a progressive deliverance occurred. After finding Jesus Christ, the Holy Spirit became my great Psychiatrist and the light of God began to shine on and bring healing to the dark areas of my personality.

Romans 12:2 says: "And do not be conformed to this world, but be transformed by the renewing of your mind, that you may prove what the will of God is, that which is good, acceptable and perfect." The Holy Spirit and the Word of God have the power to renew us in the spirit of our minds. Addictions, generational curses, and other bondages can be broken by the supernatural power of God.

Ephesians 4:22-24 says:

> That, in reference to your former manner of life, you lay aside the old self, which is being corrupted in accordance with the lusts of deceit, and that you be renewed in the spirit of your mind, and put on the new self, which in the likeness of God has been created in righteousness, and the holiness of truth.

UNDERSTANDING CODEPENDENCY

Many of us have been deeply hurt as children—rejected, ignored, abandoned, and in some cases molested. Such abuse causes deep psychological traumas that do not simply disappear but continue to produce damaging consequences during adulthood.

In her best-seller, *Codependent No More*, Melody Beattie concerns herself with low self-worth in regards to alcoholism codependency, but she could very well be talking about anyone suffering deep inner wounds. She writes that people of low self-worth:

- Come from troubled, repressed, and dysfunctional families.

- Deny their family was troubled, repressed, or dys-
  functional.
- Blame themselves for everything.
- Pick on themselves for everything, including the
  way they think feel, look, act, and behave.
- Become angry, defensive, self-righteous, and indig-
  nant when others blame and criticize the code-
  pendents—something codependents regularly
  do to themselves.
- Reject compliments or praise.
- Get depressed from a lack of compliments and
  praise (stroke deprivation).
- Feel different than the rest of the world.
- Think they're not quite good enough.
- Feel guilty about spending money on themselves
  or doing unnecessary or fun things for them-
  selves.
- Fear rejection.
- Take things personally.
- Have been victims of sexual, physical, or emotion-
  al abuse; neglect, abandonment, or alcoholism.
- Feel like victims.
- Tell themselves they can't do anything right.
- Are afraid of making mistakes.
- Wonder why they have a tough time making deci-
  sions.
- Expect themselves to do everything perfectly.
- Wonder why they can't get anything done to their
  satisfaction.
- Have a lot of "shoulds."
- Feel a lot of guilt.

- Feel ashamed of who they are.
- Think their lives are not worth living.

It is worth repeating that although Melody Beattie was outlining characteristics of codependents, they also would apply to many other kinds of people.

Though accepting Christ as your Lord and Savior does not cause all of your problems to magically disappear, the Christian believer has access to great power that will help him deal with these problems and overcome them.

If you find yourself described in any of the above characteristics, have every confidence that, in Christ, you can have the victory.

37

HOW TO GET YOUR EMOTIONS UNDER CONTROL

Often in life's circumstances our emotions go completely haywire. We find ourselves involved in circumstances beyond our control and, as a result, we feel angry and confused. However, our frustration and anger will not really help us in such situations. In fact, these uncontrolled emotions will actually hurt us. First, thoughts of anger trip chemical switches in our brains which create a kind of mental overdrive which begins to burn us out. Second, although they can lead us to take specific action if channeled properly, emotions still must be managed and kept under control.

Before the fall, Adam and Eve's human emotions were under the control of their spirits which were one with God. This, in turn, reflected their relationship with Him. The only emotions Adam and Eve knew were peace, tranquility, joy, a sense of adventure, discovery, creativity, love, peace, and power, as they walked with

God. But after the fall, such emotions as fear, anger, discouragement, anxiety, depression, uncertainty, and confusion became a part of their lives.

As we move through Earth School, each of us is going to regularly experience a full range of positive and negative emotions. It is normal to experience positive and negative emotions in this life. We're never going to live on some spiritual cloud where emotions are non-existent. However, the person whose mind is renewed will not be under the control of his or her emotions and subjected to their whims. With the renewal of our minds, then our emotions come under the Lordship of Christ and the power of the kingdom integrates itself into our emotional life.

Thus, when fears loom in our minds, we can allow the light of Christ to dispel them. Christ's mind in us reorients our perspective so that we see the potential problem through God's ability to miraculously provide for us. The emotion of fear comes into our consciousness because—as part of the mental state produced by the fall—we realize that on our own we do not have the resources, strength, power, or wisdom to meet every challenge. Earth School will present constant situations to teach us that we cannot make it on our own and we need God's help. This is one of the purposes of Earth School—to teach us that life is impossible to live without God.

The good part is that—when we begin to look at problems through God's eyes and recognize that our resources, power, strength, and wisdom are not in ourselves, but in Him—the miracle of personal transformation occurs.

We come to understand that no problem is too difficult for God to solve. At that moment we are free and the power of God begins to flow into the situation.

The reason our emotions get out of control is because they stem not from a renewed mind, but a fallen one. God's purpose in renewing our minds is to induce us to think with the mind of Christ. This allows Jesus to be Lord of our emotions and minds. We then can begin to live from a position of power and wholeness. We do not suppress our emotions and deny them. We allow them to be reintegrated with the mind of Christ and the Holy Spirit, to allow the light of God to come into the darkness.

As the absence of light is darkness, so spiritual darkness is simply the absence of God's light in a place or situation. When God's light is allowed to be present, then all things come under divine order, which always produces peace, healing, love, abundance, grace, and creativity.

Below, on the left side of the page, is a list of emotional states which are negative products of the fallen mind. When we reintegrate these negative emotions with the mind of Christ and allow God's light to permeate them, they are transformed into the positive emotional states of the renewed mind listed on the right.

When we allow God's light—through prayer, praise, and worship—to be shed on our various situations, the kingdom comes into our circumstances and the heavy burdens of emotional tyranny are lifted by the One who says, "My burden is easy and My yoke is light."

175

<u>THE FALLEN MIND</u>   <u>THE RENEWED MIND</u>

Fear .... Faith
Anxiety .... Peace
Confusion .... Clear thinking
Apprehension........................... Boldness
Lust .... Healthy desire
Hate .... Love
Anger .... Trust
Depression .... Joy
Dullness .... Creativity
Cynicism.................................. Positivism
Doubt .... Power
Loneliness .... Fellowship and
                                        communion
Emptiness .... Overflowing
Bitterness .... Thankfulness

When the light of God's kingdom is brought to bear on the human mind and spirit, a healing and transformation takes place which makes a person whole.

DON'T BE LED ASTRAY BY FEELINGS

Feelings are the product of our personalities reacting to outside stimuli or internal thoughts. Feelings are illusory and often fleeting. Although feelings can be positive, they are not something on which you can build your life. A spiritual person can never be ruled by feelings. What should govern our lives is faith in God's Word.

Emotions come and go; one minute we can be on top of the world and the next we are in the dumps. Circumstances or a careless remark can deeply depress us. In Hebrews 11:1, we read, "Now faith is the substance of things hoped for and the evidence of things not seen." This means that our belief and trust in God and the promises of His Word should rule over our feelings. We must believe God whether we feel like it or not.

This does not mean that we become robots or lose our capacity for spontaneity. It simply means we are no longer to be emotionally out of control. We are to live our lives believing and trusting God, regardless of our feelings. This is part of the process of abiding with Jesus and it is the place of total victory.

Our inner spirit begins to rule over our emotions, they come under control of the Holy Spirit and have a calming effect on us. We walk in praise and worship before our King. When we do this, we will find that peace and joy begin to spring forth despite our outward circumstances.

38

HOW TO BREAK THE CURSE OF
EATING DISORDERS

Eating disorders plague a large segment of our population, from the more than six million Americans who are twenty percent overweight to the tens of millions with minor weight problems, anorexia nervosa, and other food-related problems. Many people use food to deal with stress, emotional pain, and depression.

In her book *Fat is A Family Affair*, Judi Hollis writes,

...In the early 1970's, doctors studied a mechanism within the nervous system which produces a morphine-like effect helping to alleviate pain and subduing trauma and shock. These morphine-like substances are called endorphins and they are secreted to soothe pain, take the edge off, and promote general well being. Some research indicates that overeaters and alcoholics produce fewer of these endorphins than normal people ... Since you produce fewer endorphins, you often feel on a raw edge. Eating sugar increases endorphin production, so when you eat the rawness vanishes... If anorexic, you get the same kind of soothing from the "high" of not eating. That exuberant feeling comes from the endurance high of pushing yourself beyond your limits, much like the "runner's high...."

It appears many people with eating disorders are in reality medicating themselves by changing their body chemistry. People addicted to sweets and chocolates are in reality giving themselves a dose of a biochemical drug that gives them a subtle high. The same is true concerning eating carbohydrates like pasta or the concentration of an amino acid—tryptophan—in turkey, cheese, and milk. The pleasant, euphoric feeling gained from drinking warm milk at night or having a big turkey dinner comes from the amino acid tryptophan contained in these foods. It is an ironic fact that a great deal of biochemical tampering and internal drugs created by eating certain foods goes on that is just as addictive, though less destructive, than alcohol and illegal drugs.

The finger of condemnation should not be pointed at people with such food addictions, because eating is a means by which they deal with emotional pain and stress. Healing is needed in all such cases, and even though it is probably less harmful to be addicted to chocolate than to drugs, both addictions are bad for your health and indicative of emotional bondage.

The cure for eating disorders is found in the same process for breaking the generational curse in any area. The solution lies in allowing the Holy Spirit to reach deep within our personalities and heal the wounds and fragmentations of our persons. First Thessalonians 5:23 states; "Now may the God of peace Himself sanctify you entirely; and may your spirit and soul and body be preserved complete, without blame at the coming of our Lord Jesus Christ."

The word sanctify means to set apart or make holy or whole. God wants our spirits, souls, and bodies to be made whole until the coming of our Lord. He can pour His Spirit into our empty lives and fill deep emotional needs we now seek to satisfy in other ways. Worship is so important for the believer, for when we learn and experience true worship, we find ourselves filled to overflowing with His Spirit. We are then no longer empty and seeking fulfillment or have a need to be filled through food, drugs, alcohol, and other things. The addictive personality is found in a person with unmet needs. Once the Lord—by the power of the Holy Spirit—begins to fill those needs, we learn how to worship Jesus Christ in spirit and truth. The addictive personality is then no longer addicted to things. The addiction—or emotional, spiritual, and psychological allegiance—has been transferred to God.

The Spirit of the Lord springs up like a fountain from a person's soul—from a place of power, joy, and delight—flooding it with the indescribable presence of Jesus Christ which intoxicates with a supernatural heavenly joy that those outside Christ simply cannot know unless they turn their hearts to Him.

39

HOW TO REVERSE THE CURSE

Ultimately all generational curses and problems we face are anchored in the root problem of the sin that entered into the human race when Adam and Eve chose to disobey God. This does not negate the importance of personal choice and will, but very clearly indicates that sin, as an all-encompassing death force, is very much at work in the world. But thank God there is a more powerful life force at work on our planet in Jesus Christ. That gives us the personal choice of accepting the consequences of sin or placing our faith in Jesus and being moved into the stream of eternal life.

Disease, destruction, poverty, sickness, fear, depression, alcoholism, occult bondage, sexual problems, anger, poor self-image, and many other conditions all have their source in sin. This is passed down through the generations by genetics, psychological conditioning, or as a spirit. However, God has made salvation available through Jesus Christ and it is possible to *Reverse the Curse.*

We no longer have to be trapped by powerful negative forces which we cannot control. We're not actors performing on the stage of life with scripts containing the seeds of our own destruction. Jesus Christ has the power to heal, save, and deliver you. The Savior brings the awesome power to transform us right now. The same power that resurrected Jesus Christ from the dead and performed the many miracles we read in the Gospels is available to you!

Paul's letter to the Romans describes the Christian view of the human condition. It clearly and precisely outlines the reality of sin and how destructive it can be for the individual. But it does not stop there. The Apostle Paul points to the way of freedom and release from inner bondage, summing it up with: "For in it the righteousness of God is revealed from faith to faith; as it is written, *but the righteous man shall live by faith*" (Rom. 1:17 italics mine).

Faith in Jesus Christ is the key, for it is the faith in salvation brought by the Lord which has the power to break any bondages we may have. The secret of deliverance is wrapped up in knowing that we do not have the power to save ourselves, but that power is available through Jesus Christ.

This is the sin of mankind, and of humanism, which falsely and pridefully believes that man has the power to save himself. The mad rush for scientific achievement, political realignment, and personal power will ultimately deliver much less than it promises. Mankind needs a

Savior. You and I need a savior. We are finite individuals who will either bow our heads before our Creator in faith in Christ, bringing on salvation, or we will bow at the day of judgment.

The Scriptures state: "For all have sinned and fall short of the glory of God" (Rom. 3:23). The question is, how do we get out from under the curse mankind is under due to the fall in the Garden of Eden? It is easy to believe that living a moral life and doing good works is enough. But the Gospel of Jesus Christ, or true biblical Christianity, does not say this. In Romans 4:3: "For what does the Scripture say? 'And Abraham believed God, and it was reckoned to him as righteousness.'" In the Old Testament God tells us that salvation comes from having faith in the promises of God, not through good works. True salvation from God comes as a free and unearned gift. Simply have faith in Christ and receive Him as your personal Savior and, as a result, you will have a right relationship with God in this life and eternal life with Him in the next.

We can only find wholeness through faith in Jesus Christ and His power to heal. When sin is at work in the human personality, it is like quicksand—the more you struggle, the deeper you sink. You can only be rescued by reaching out in faith to Jesus Christ and allowing Him to pull you out.

God understands the conflict that wages war in your personality. In Romans 7:15-21, it reads:

> For that which I am doing, I do not understand;
> for I am not practicing what I would like to do,

but I am doing the very thing I hate. But if I do the very thing I do not wish to do, I agree with the Law, confessing that it is good. So now, no longer am I the one doing it, but sin which indwells me. For I know that nothing good dwells in me, that is, in my flesh; for the wishing is present in me, but the doing of the good is not. For the good that I wish, I do not do; but I practice the very evil that I do not wish. But if I am doing the very thing I do not wish, I am no longer the one doing it, but sin which dwells in me. I find then the principle that evil is present in me, the one who wishes to do good.

The insight of the Apostle Paul enlightens us concerning a powerful dynamic of human behavior. We can desire to do good and yet find ourselves doing the very thing we do not want to do. Paul tells us that the cause of this is sin dwelling in us, against which we alone are powerless. But Christ has the power to set us free even from this, and we can always be confident that this power is available to us, as long as we continue to walk in His ways.

40

BUILDING A NEW SELF-IMAGE

One of the prime keys to healing the generational curse is to build a new self-image. If we come from dysfunctional families, we unconsciously model that behavior as adults.

If we find ourselves trapped in a mind set of fear, indecisiveness, poverty consciousness, and any number of negative behaviors, the only way we can be free of them is to learn new and more positive behaviors.

In Romans 12:2 (KJV) the Apostle Paul says, "And be not conformed to this world, but be ye transformed by the renewing of your mind...." How do we do this? We begin to think as God thinks and we do this by studying His Word. Thus, through repetition, prayer, and commitment, we train our minds to think in accordance with the Scriptures.

Some practical steps to take to renew your mind:

Step One: Begin to see yourself as God sees you. "I pray that the eyes of your heart may be enlightened, so that you may know what is the hope of His calling, what are the riches of the glory of His inheritance in the saints" (Eph. 1:18). God sees us as saints, persons who have a great cosmic destiny. You must allow yourself to dream of what God created you to be no matter how difficult or dark your present earthly struggle is. You are a person of great destiny, whether you feel like it or not. In addition, through God's grace and power you must begin to grow in that destiny.

Step Two: You must know the promises of God for you in His Word. Society, family, and circumstances should not ultimately define who you are. God has a destiny for you that He has written about in His Word, which you must read; you must also claim His promises for your life. In Psalms 37:4 it says, "Delight yourself in the Lord; and He will give you the desires of your heart." There are hundreds of promises from God to you in the Bible. You need to know them to succeed.

Step Three: You cannot allow the generational curse of fear to define who you are. Fear of failure or any other images rooted in fear cannot have a place in your mind. It says in Second Timothy 1:7 (KJV), "For God has not given us a spirit of fear; but of power, and of love, and of a sound mind." Fear can limit us and keep us from God's best if we allow it to do so. We cannot allow fear to shape our futures. We must renounce the spirit of fear in our lives by using the authority of Jesus Christ and, by faith, we must see ourselves through the eyes of faith.

Step Four: We must see ourselves through the eyes of faith and not allow our present circumstances to determine who we are. We must truly see what God is doing and can do with our lives. We must fight the good fight of faith. God did not create us to be burned out and washed up.

Step Five: Discover the dream God placed within you. God has placed a dream in our hearts—a dream of restored personality, a healed marriage, or a blessed career. We must move boldly toward it. We must dare to dream the same dream God has already dreamed for us. "Surely there is a future, and your hope will not be cut off" (Prov. 23:18).

Step Six: Begin to act, look, dress, and think like the person you want to become. You already are that person, but fear and conditioning may have hidden that fact from you. Step out and be the person you want to become. Just wake up and do it! Our personalities are not fixed. God has allowed us creative power over our own lives. However, we must use that power. "...In the name of Jesus Christ the Nazarene...walk!" (Acts 3:6)

Step Seven: Don't allow discouragement to crush your dream. Don't allow failure, sins, or discouragement to prevent you from becoming all that God has for you. Remember you have an enemy who wants to destroy you. Discouragement is his prime weapon. If you have failed at something, learn from your mistakes and start again. If it looks hopeless, it isn't; it's never hopeless in Christ. See it through the eyes of faith. No matter what it feels like, keep on keeping on. "Forgetting those things that are behind me I reach for the mark of the high calling in Christ Jesus."

GENERATIONAL BLESSING

As well as generational curses, so too are blessings passed on from one generation to another. In Genesis 27:27-29 we read the account of Isaac blessing his son:

> See, the smell of my son is like the smell of the field which the Lord has blessed; now may God give you the dew of heaven, and of the fatness of the earth, and an abundance of grain and new wine; may peoples serve you, and nations bow down to you; be master of your brothers, and may your mother's sons bow down to you. Cursed be those who curse you, and blessed be those who bless you.

In the Bible, a blessing is a release of spiritual power and favor in someone's life which has tangible and measurable results. Here we see the account of how Jacob contrived to literally steal his brother Esau's blessing. He did this because he knew how valuable this blessing would be to him in the future, and he would stop at nothing to get it.

The Bible tells us that blessing and not curses are passed down the generations for those who live godly lives and love God and especially for those who have accepted Christ and walk with Him.

BLESSING IN ACTION

On a June Sunday in 1991, Kristina and I went to have our baby, Paul Christopher, dedicated by our pastor Rev.

Jack Hayford of The Church On The Way. After the dedication, Pastor Jack taught on the power of blessing for believers. He called Kris and me up to the platform to use as an illustration of how every believer has the authority to bless others.

Pastor Jack laid hands on us and prayed this prayer of blessing, "Father God, I bless Paul and Kris in the name of Jesus. I bless them with wisdom in their parental responsibility. I bless them with abundance according to your Word. I bless them, Lord, with anointing for the task you have given them. Paul and Kris, in the name of the Most High God may His blessing be upon you. His covering mantle of abundance and grace surround you through Jesus our Lord, Amen."

Pastor Jack went on to point out that his authority to bless us was not because he was a pastor, but his authority was based upon the fact that he was of the seed of Abraham. He went on to point out that every believer can do this. "I will bless those who bless you and you will be a blessing." Pastor Hayford taught that morning that every believer in Christ has the power to ask God's blessing on others.

I believe in the power of blessing. I have seen firsthand God's supernatural force at work to cause good things to happen in my life, and the lives of others, that transcends any logical explanation. Divine protection, miracles, provision, and answered prayer have invaded my world and the world of others too many times for me to count.

41

HOW TO BE CURED OF INNER PAIN

Deep within every person who is honest enough to admit it, there is much pain. This is not necessarily pain from loss of a loved one, career dissatisfaction, or the like. We each have great reservoirs of pain, stored up since childhood, to go along with the hurts of everyday life. We will continuously have to deal with pain during our life on planet Earth. Only in our real home, which is heaven, will we find complete rest.

Each of us has varying degrees of inner pain—some more, some less, intensified by such painful events and circumstances as divorce, deaths, injury, rejection, or abuse. We deal with inner pain in different ways, including denial, fantasy, eating, alcohol, drugs, pornography, psychotherapy, meditation, and escapism. All these and more, whether good or bad, can be used to try to alleviate inner pain.

But this inner pain can only be eased by coming to God, our caring and loving Heavenly Father. It is only God, through His Son Jesus Christ, who is capable of bearing our burdens. When we can come to God, He will lift the pain from us, or give us the strength to endure it.

In practical terms this is accomplished by coming to God in prayer. What is prayer? Prayer is simply talking to God. We can talk to Him as we would a close friend. The pain we carry can be soothed by talking to Jesus Christ. Then we can feel the presence of the Holy Spirit mending our hearts. In God's presence, which we need to find, there is always healing. We enter His presence through worship and praise in a church, car, or the privacy of our homes. Even while reading this book, we can open our hearts to God's presence and He will reach into the depths of our souls and heal the inner torment.

Jesus is alive. He is alive with you at this very moment. He is your friend as well as your Lord. His compassion knows no bounds. Allow the love of God to fill you to overflowing. Allow the river of life to replenish and renew you. God is real and He can touch you right now where you are. Let Him heal you. Let Jesus mend your past as well as your present and future.

Despite the pain, let the praise well up in your heart with thanksgiving. Thank God for His goodness, and let the balm of Gilead caress your inner being.

God is intimate with us and loves us as no human being can. He is on our side and desires the best for us. Do we understand that God loves us? The words that God speaks to us minister life. Words without life—no

Christian word ever returns empty—can minister only death.

By the Holy Spirit, God sends us the healing flow of His power and love. The river of life heals us as we come in contact with it, and the human personality is mended and restored. Jesus is the source of that river, and you can find healing by simply opening up to Christ's love.

If I can share one thought with you, the reader, it is that true and complete inner healing can only come from God; psychological formulas or technique will not suffice. This is not to denigrate the importance of human agencies, but only God can mend the broken spirit and give wholeness. Inner healing will occur if you open up to Jesus at the deepest dimensions of your personality. My prayer is that you be blessed when you read this and the Spirit of Christ imparts wholeness to you. Then rejoicing will come, for God's healing and deliverance invariably produces joy. This is what God has for you. Walk in confidence with Him.

42

REMEMBERING YOUR CHILDHOOD

Who you are as an adult is a reflection of who you were as a child. Loneliness, rejection, insecurity, and fear are typical of feelings that may be rooted in specific events in your past.

It is important to remember your feelings about how your parents treated you. A way to identify the influence your past has on your present is to write down a list of things troubling you as an adult, then make a comparable list of the feelings you had as a child. If you compare the lists, you will see a remarkable similarity between the two.

First, write a list of problems you are struggling with now. Here are some common adult problems:

1. Fear of rejection.
2. Feelings of inadequacy, such as not being smart enough, attractive enough, not well liked, incapable of completing a job, etc.

3. Too much concern about what people think of you.
4. Always trying to win other people's approval by perfectionism.
5. Excessively adapting your behavior and personality to be accepted by other people (people pleasing).
6. Fear of authority figures such as pastors, policemen, bosses, etc.
7. Fear of being found out as a phony, or that if people really got to know you, they wouldn't like you.

Now match your current list of problems with a list of how you felt as a child:

1. You felt unwanted by your parents and that they didn't really love you (rejection).
2. Your parents were over-critical and made you feel you didn't measure up to their standards. They did not compliment you when you did something right, did not make you feel secure or build your self-esteem, and they left you with the feeling that you just weren't good enough, even though you may have tried very hard to earn their acceptance.
3. You thought your parents didn't love you very much, and you wondered what was wrong with you that made them feel this way.
4. Consequently, because you did not feel accepted, you tried to earn people's approval by being as

perfect as you could be. You felt if you got top grades in school, dressed right, or whatever, people would love you.

5. Since you thought of yourself as an inadequate oddball, you tried to change your personality to be accepted. If your parents or friends wanted you to act or be a certain way, that's how you acted. Maybe you were the class clown, the star athlete, or the big brain; in any case, you found yourself adapting your personality for acceptance to such a point that you lost the sense of who you really were.

6. You were afraid of your father. He was cold, distant, and critical.

7. Rejection by either, or both, parents made you feel unlovable, although you could never really pinpoint what it was that made you that way. This made you feel unworthy, and you feared someone would find out what it was about you that was unlovable.

The basic human personality is shaped during childhood. Matching up the two lists should give you a direct correlation between your childhood feelings and your perceptions with present-day problems. For example, if your parents did not love and accept you or build your self-esteem, you may as an adult have problems with feelings of insecurity or lack of self-worth. You may, as a result, tend to excessively seek approval from others.

It is clearly helpful to understand the relationship between childhood experiences and adult problems. Gaining such knowledge is the first step on the road to healing. Now you must take a further step.

LEARNING HOW TO THINK AND FEEL

Once causes of certain adult psychological problems are identified, the next step is learning how to use this knowledge to bring about healing. A lifetime of work may be required. There are no easy answers, magic cure-alls, or one-time miraculous prayers that will instantaneously provide a cure. God can and will perform miracles and empower you to overcome this negative conditioning, which will enable you to succeed through the Holy Spirit. But there is going to be a lot of work, commitment, and discipline involved.

If your parents were critical of you, did not make you feel secure, or build your self-esteem, when you're at a business meeting or a party, you may become very nervous and afraid. It's as if a tape were playing through your mind, and you find yourself thinking, "They probably won't like me;" "they'll think I'm stupid, or out of it," or any number of self-deprecating thoughts. Subconsciously, you are putting yourself down because of your childhood experience with overly-critical parents.

But, now you are ready to take a bold, new step. You choose to stop being victimized by the past. You are going to start thinking differently and begin to see yourself as God wants you to be.

The moment negative thoughts arise, you say to yourself, "No! I am respectable and likeable and intelligent."

Your right to say this is because you have allowed a personal revelation of God's Word to enter your heart, which you choose to believe in spite of your childhood experiences. God loves you; you must be worthy of love and respect if the Creator of the universe loves you.

A great weight can be lifted off when you apply this principle. However, you can't fake it. You must really believe what God says about you, and act on that belief. You must come to a true understanding of who you are in Christ. And if you really understand that Christianity is TRUTH, and that the true God loves you personally beyond measure, then you can live in that reality. When you have done your intellectual homework, when you have thought it through completely, when you really understand who Christ is and who you are in Christ, then healing can take place.

The goal is to become aware of your thoughts and perceptions, and deal with them appropriately. In every thought relating to your situations, you must allow the reality of God's truth to come to bear. You are a new creation in Christ—no longer fearful, insecure, stupid, or lacking in talent and ability. In Christ you have access to many resources, and you are now more than a conqueror!

43

MONITORING YOUR THOUGHTS

If you want to know what is going on deep inside you, then I suggest you spend a day monitoring your thoughts, especially while interacting with other people. This will reveal a wealth of information about yourself. The goal is to be aware of your thought processes. Let's look at some examples:

1. You meet with your boss and are afraid he doesn't like or approve of you, even though you have done an outstanding job.
2. At a social gathering you let loose a little, crack jokes, and let people see more of you than normally. You drop your guard and let people acquaint themselves with your real self. Yet you walk away barraged with thoughts about how they feel about you. Do they think you are odd or stupid? You are very critical of your own behavior.

3. Driving home alone, you beat up on yourself emotionally. You critically attack yourself for everything you've done that is less than perfect.
4. Your employer tells you what a fantastic job you've done and praises you for this fine accomplishment. But you really don't believe what your employer said, and the next day you are again doubting yourself.
5. Though people may consider you very successful, you feel inwardly that if they really knew you, they would be disappointed.
6. During a discussion your spouse makes a criticism and you fly off the handle, taking it far more seriously then it was meant.
7. Invited to speak before a group, you are terrified because you feel that people will be extremely critical of you. You also find yourself very critical of other people.

The list could go on, but the point is, these and other thoughts reveal a great deal about you. And such thoughts are not accidental, but probably occur often—although you may not always be aware of them. They stem from patterns developed in early childhood that have now become automatic.

We must become aware of our thoughts, for they indicate what is going on beneath the surface of our personalities. These are unconscious energies, driving us and causing us to act certain ways. The root of all these thoughts expressed in the above examples is a poor self-image and early childhood rejection. Such thoughts come from people who were rejected by their parents and, as a result, question their own self-worth. Thus, the insecurity and poor self-image interferes with a person's ability to experience a normal, happy, and productive adult life.

Mere intellectual understanding of this dynamic does not mean we will be healed, even though we now know why we think in certain ways. Such knowledge does not automatically heal us from feeling rejected, insecure, and having a poor self-image. We must emotionally and spiritually experience on a very deep level what it means to be really loved and accepted. Then the healing will begin.

Jesus Christ can perform this miracle for you. He can heal the deep wounds and make you feel loved to the depths of your being. He will, however, most often give you that embrace through other people—friend, pastor, spouse, or fellow Christian.

If we come to God in prayer and give our hurt and pain to Him, we will find the deep, inner, emotional release we are looking for. Husbands and wives must be agents of God's love and healing to each other, as are all Christians. Sometimes when the love of Jesus Christ is so real and we are really touched by God, deep inner bondages are broken and released. The fearful, hurting child inside cries when embraced, and for the first time you know you are really loved.

44

HOW TO TALK TO YOURSELF

It is not only important how we talk to others, but also how we talk to ourselves. These deep, inner conversations we have when nobody else is around can make or break us.

Successful people in life have somehow mastered the art of talking to themselves. They can forgive, build up, or encourage themselves. On the other hand, failures usually beat up on, set impossible standards for, and criticize themselves unmercifully.

Successful people I know have learned to talk to themselves in a positive, uplifting manner. Instead of beating up on themselves, they have learned how to build themselves up.

What you say to yourself is powerful for good or ill. If you ruthlessly rehearse every mistake you have made during the day, and tar and feather yourself for all these errors, you are going to be tired, depressed, and downtrodden.

Pounding yourself into the ground is a destructive activity that will leave you in no shape to succeed in any pursuit. Thus, you will be unsuccessful, and have every reason to criticize yourself for failing.

Instead, if you build up and encourage yourself, you will have the energy and inner belief system to succeed and overcome external obstacles. Life and other people will give you enough negative criticism and feedback without you having to do it to yourself.

THE FAMILY AS A SYSTEM

John Bradshaw, author of *The Family*, recently did an excellent PBS television series on the concept of the family as a system. Bradshaw's background of drinking alcoholically from early teens to age 30 helped him to identify what is now termed "the dysfunctional family." During the lecture, Bradshaw stood next to a metal mobile which hung from the ceiling on thin wires. Using this visual aid, he demonstrated how unbalanced a whole family can become if any one member is out of balance due to alcoholism, eating disorders, workaholism, sexual addictions, etc.

This scenario shows how the dysfunctional family practices forms of denial to protect the compulsive behavior of one member. For instance a workaholic trying to camouflage inner shame and personal inadequacy may sublimate his or her depression through work. But the son or daughter may end up carrying that depression.

The World Health Organization defines compulsiveness as a "pathological relationship to a mood altering event, experience or thing that has life damaging consequences." People can become addicted to sex, food, religion, drugs, alcohol, hobbies, or even Monday Night Football in order to deal with the pain and emptiness within. Sometimes these things are not harmful if done in moderation or within the right framework. But anything, including work or eating, can become an addiction when turned into compulsive behavior. Even Christian activity can be compulsive, if used as an escape or avoidance mechanism in dealing with problems God wants us to face.

A family with its interlocking systems of relationships can be a center of tremendous joy and healing. These days, however, American families are too often sick, dysfunctional, and riddled with compulsive behaviors. The root cause of these disorders is spiritual emptiness.

For every alcoholic, there are six or seven people in the average family system affected in a negative way by the compulsive drinking. Organizations such as Adult Children of Alcoholics (ACOA) are among the fastest growing, because they attempt to deal with the pain and suffering brought on by families dysfunctional from the widespread abuse of alcohol.

Children learn to adapt themselves to the compulsive behaviors of their parents in order to survive. The child in the alcoholism or drug-ridden home must learn adult responsibilities to compensate for the addicted grown-up's out-of-control and irresponsible behavior. Such children must do a lot of people-pleasing in order to get past the mood swings of the impaired parent. In the process, they become out of touch and isolated from their own true feelings. This creates problems later on in the adult years—problems that are brought into the marriage or workplace.

Children in dysfunctional families "introject" judgmental scripts in their minds which carry into their adult years. As an example, rejection by parents who have no time for nurturing translates into the child's beginning to question his or her worth. This "introjection" turns into deep inner shame which the child develops compulsive behaviors around in order to erase it.

All compulsions are a way to manage emotions or to make you feel alive. Sexual perversions, such as use of pornography, child molestation, homosexuality, and extramarital affairs, are means to deal with inner pain. As do alcohol and drugs, these behaviors, even if they are pathological, give a momentary feeling of excitement. It is here the powers of darkness can enter into the compulsion and create real havoc and bondage.

Most sexual addictions are limited to viewing pornography and having affairs, both of which can become like a drug to the compulsive individual. Womanizing men and promiscuous women use sex as a means to escape inner pain and inner shame. Tragically, this cyclical behavior increases shame immediately after the excitement subsides. To escape this feeling of shame, the person must then seek a new sexual experience to get back the drug-like high. Christians and non-Christians alike often seek sexual excitement as a substitute for true intimacy.

Our culture is currently in a crisis of compulsion—a crisis propelled and fueled by a mass media attempting to exploit those compulsions through consumerism. We do not instantly become immune to these problems once we become Christians, nor do we instantly receive healing from our family problems of the past. We must walk with Christ and work out these problems throughout our lifetime. This requires self-honesty, prayer, faith, and hard work.

45

THE NATURE OF YOUR BATTLE

Like it or not, you are in a struggle against unseen powers in the invisible realm. If you are making spiritual progress and are an effective witness for Christ, you are going to experience intense opposition from the enemy. Every sincere Christian must expect this.

The great war between God and Satan is still going on, even as you read this book. It is taking place in our individual lives, families, cities, and nation. It is the responsibility of the believer in Jesus Christ to be constantly alert and in daily prayer regarding our lives and the lives of others.

"Be of sober spirit, be on the alert. Your adversary, the devil, prowls about like a roaring lion, seeking someone to devour" (1 Peter 5:8). As individuals and as a nation, we are often oblivious to the schemes of the devil. The reason we are at a time of great immorality is precisely because the Christian Church has been neglecting its mission. We were not praying and being responsible stewards of our society. Many of society's problems today are because of our inactivity and our failure to take seriously our responsibilities as Christians and as citizens.

Yet if we think the same danger does not exist in our lives as individuals, then we are deceived. We must be constantly armed with the power of the Holy Spirit. "Submit therefore to God. Resist the devil and he will flee from you" (James 4:7). In First Peter 1:13 we read: "Therefore, gird your minds for action, keep sober in spirit...." We live in a hostile environment where invisible beings are attempting to dislodge, confuse, hinder, and destroy us. If we are apathetic and spiritually dull, the enemy can strike while our guard is down.

The mass media constantly barrages us with ideas and messages contrary to the message of the Gospel. Co-workers can do and say things that hurt and anger us. Family members can oppress, accidents can mysteriously happen, strange temptations, and opportunities to sin can present themselves without warning. Anything can happen at any time.

This discussion is not to create a state of fear and paranoia. Its purpose is to forewarn and prepare you for attacks by the enemy in your life. There are things we can do to supernaturally protect ourselves and our loved ones, as well as our communities, cities, and nation. Once we understand we are in a war zone, then it is our responsibility to marshal an adequate defense and offense. Our primary weapons are prayer, praise, and intercession. We must cover our lives, families, jobs, and all of humanity in prayer and bind the powers of darkness from operating.

What this requires is what Dr. Peter Wagner of Fuller Theological Seminary calls "Warfare Prayer." We must be actively engaged in spiritual warfare and not only binding the powers of darkness, but calling down revival, angels, and spreading the dominion of the kingdom of God.

We must take our roles as priests, intercessors, and prayer warriors seriously. Many of the things that hinder and block us come as a result of prayerlessness. Prayer is the most powerful weapon in the universe. Prayer can not only change our destiny, but the destiny of nations. Prayer should not be viewed as a drudgery, but as the most exciting thing we can do. Prayer changes things. As Rev. Jack Hayford has said, "Prayer is invading the impossible."

SATANIC OPPOSITION IN YOUR LIFE

There is a force opposing you and your family and that force is Satan and his demons. There is a force behind such events as serial killing, wars, child abuse, murder, drug addiction, greed, and corruption that is beyond mere human agency. There is a devil who has a master game plan for the destruction of the human race.

Your progress and the well-being of your family can be affected by this adversary if you allow him to attack. "The thief comes only to steal, and kill, and destroy; I come that they might have life, and might have it more abundantly" (John 10:10). God promises us an abundant life, but we also must be on guard against a thief who comes to steal, kill and destroy. Remember, a thief does not come when you are prepared, but seeks his opportunity when you are off guard.

The enemy will attempt to destroy us in subtle ways. There are numerous incidents in my life where the devil has attacked me because I was not vigilant. I can recall at least two occasions when, although I was walking with the Lord, going to church, and reading the Bible, I still had let my guard down. I falsely assumed that I was in control and that I was really spiritual and therefore safe. It was at these times that the devil attacked me with temptation, calamity, and oppression.

The Bible warns us to be sober and vigilant "Be of sober spirit, be on alert. Your adversary, the devil, prowls about like a roaring lion, seeking someone to devour" (1 Peter 5:8). Unexplained sicknesses, sudden financial problems, marital upheavals, attacks on your children, temptations, and pressures loom up from everywhere. Any one or all of these can be an attack by the devil.

My wife, child, and I spent Christmas day with some friends in Beverly Hills. I was driving home in my Toyota Celica, which was equipped with a driver-side air bag. My baby boy was in the infant seat in front and my wife was driving another car home. I hate to admit it, but I was cruising in the fast lane between seventy and eighty miles per hour, going downhill on the I-5 Freeway near Valencia. My son was asleep and I was listening to the radio. Because everything was going so well, I had let my guard down.

Ahead of me was a big Ford Bronco, also making good time. Suddenly it pulled into the right lane—and I was looking at a car with its lights aimed right at me, coming from about two hundred feet ahead.

Time seemed to slow down. I couldn't go right because the Bronco was blocking me. I couldn't go left because of a divider which separated me from a downhill drop of at least one hundred feet. In just seconds, I would smash the onrushing car. I knew my air bag would be useless to protect my son. I mentally envisaged the awful wreckage of two cars colliding at eighty miles per hour. Suddenly, I hit the brakes and pulled to safety in the right lane, which just as suddenly was miraculously empty.

The incident was so frighteningly close, for days I had flashbacks of the scene running through my mind. I knew God himself had pulled me to safety at the last second, and that my son and I have a purpose in life. I knew the angels of God had rescued me. I learned a powerful lesson and I now try to drive no faster than the legal limit.

Using my own negligence, the thief tried to kill me and my son. I let my guard down and he struck with lightning speed. But I had prayed many times with my wife for our protection on the freeway, asking the angels of God to be with us in binding incidents. I believe at that moment God answered with protection. Disaster was diverted because of prayer.

We believers in Jesus Christ are under attack from an unseen world and we need daily to pray and wear the full armor of God. A number of years before the near accident with my son I was driving my wife, who at that time was an actress, to her agent's office on Santa Monica Boulevard. She was crossing the street while I waited in the car for her return. Suddenly I heard a loud screech of tires. I didn't think about it until I saw a large crowd gathering and heard a young man say, "Man! Did you see that girl fly up over the car!" I ran across the street to discover my wife had been hit by a Cadillac and thrown up over the hood onto the sidewalk. Miraculously she was not hurt, because she was thrown over the car and not under it. When I reached her, she was praising God out loud and talking about the angels protecting her. I grabbed her, thinking she was in shock, but she was just being thankful for God's intervention!

Of course, auto accidents are not the only means of assault. But as believers in Christ, if we pray for God's protection daily, we can withstand the assaults.

I believe this need for protection should include regularly anointing our loved ones with oil and praying for them. As members of The Church On The Way, we receive little vials of healing oil. We use ours constantly. When we moved into our new home, we anointed every door and window with oil and bound the devil and thief from coming into our home. We also marched around the inside and outside of our house praising God aloud and speaking in tongues. We felt it necessary to do a spiritual housecleaning to remove all presences not of God. We also invited the power of the Holy Spirit to fill the house always.

We have had relatives stay and comment about how peaceful and restful our house is. Peace abides in our house because we bound the power of the adversary and established the dominion of Christ upon our home.

If you take the invisible realm seriously as we do, then it is important to do this. You even have to go a couple of steps further. We also pray this prayer for our neighbors, block, and community. We bind the spirits of alcoholism, drug addiction, the occult, suicide, divorce, and enemy power of our community and ask God to send salvation and revival.

The thief will strike automatically if he is not bound. As a participant in an interdenominational prayer meeting called LOVE-LA, that meets at Hollywood Presbyterian Church, I regularly join Christian leaders in prayer for Los Angeles. Inner-city gang violence, racism, crime, and poverty are also the work of the thief. Collectively, over ten thousand Christians gathered at the Faith Dome at Crenshaw Christian Center with Rev. Hayford, Rev. Lloyd Oglivie, and Rev. Fred Price, who led an intercessory prayer rally for Los Angeles that bound the thief which comes to steal, kill, and destroy.

The key is to be sober-minded and vigilant always and to enter into spiritual warfare for yourself, family, community, city, and nation. You cannot afford the luxury of letting your guard down. Instead you must wage war against your adversary and bind the power of the thief over your life. You cannot take this for granted. Spiritual warfare is something you must constantly do because you are in daily battle.

46

HOW TO DEFEAT THE SPIRIT OF HOPELESSNESS

Inside each of us is a tremendous storehouse of gifts and potentialities. But we already know we have an enemy trying to block us from becoming all God wants us to become. Sadly, goals He would have us achieve, dreams He desires to see realized, ministries that should have prospered, and lives that should have been transformed are often thwarted and blocked because the enemy has been successful in sending a spirit of hopelessness into the situation to drive the believer into despair.

I understand the spirit of hopelessness, for I have recognized and waged war against it many times. The spirit of hopelessness is a very subtle force because it always masquerades as your own thoughts! It attacks you with full force, but hides itself by making you think it is your own realistic thoughts.

Long after I became a Christian, I began to recognize a strange depression and hopelessness that would come upon me very gradually. I never paid it any attention because the outward situation appeared hopeless and I just assumed I was being realistic about things. The truth is I was being attacked by an actual spirit from hell ministering hopelessness, defeat, and discouragement.

Years of this went by before I recognized that a specific demonic entity was attacking me. I thought I was just being depressed and needed to study God's Word, pray, and trust the Lord. I did not understand that it was a frontal assault in the invisible realm from a spirit. I first understood it as the spirit of hopelessness attacking me when I heard Rev. Jack Hayford teach on a subject entitled, "You Need To Declare War," wherein he explained how the barrage of thoughts that defeat us can have Satan as their source.

I learned that I must specifically come against this spirit in the name of Jesus Christ and take authority over it. "I kept looking, and that horn was waging war with the saints and overpowering them" (Dan. 7:21). This passage refers to the attack of Satan against God's people in the last days as well as his attacks now in the invisible realm.

The spirit of hopelessness will fix itself to your soul like a parasite and begin sucking the life out of you unless you oppose it through force. I realized I needed help to get rid of this, so while attending an annual convention of the International Church of the Foursquare Gospel in Los Angeles, I met an old friend of mine, the Rev. Tim McGill. We lunched together at a local Mexican restaurant, and I shared with him my problem of depression and hopelessness. This was unplanned, but the Holy Spirit brought it from me. My concern, my sharing, and having him pray for me distinctly severed this bondage in my personality. Supernatural deliverance from this spirit of hopelessness which had been oppressing me, happened.

To clarify a point here, I'm not talking about demonic possession. I am suggesting that believers in Jesus Christ can be attacked by specific ministering spirits. As the Body of Christ, we need to dismantle their hold over people's lives. We're all in spiritual warfare, and we're all going to be attacked. You cannot go into battle without ammunition. I have listed below the following steps that can be taken to wage war against the spirit of hopelessness, or any other spirit.

Step One: Recognize and identify your enemy as a specific spirit—hopelessness, fear, depression, lust, anger, or whatever. We are not blaming every human weakness and shortcoming on demons. However, with real discernment, we must recognize the times when we are being attacked.

Step Two: Specifically come against that spirit in the name of Jesus Christ and bind its power over your life. Command it out loud in the name of Jesus Christ to go.

Step Three: Appropriate the power of worship and praise in the face of attack. Begin worshipping and praising God for His victory, power, and protection. The enemy cannot stand being in the presence of praise and worship of God. He will flee.

Step Four: If the enemy continues to resist you, then call for reinforcements and get the help of brothers and sisters in Christ to pray with you.

Step Five: Recognize that not all battles are won instantly. The enemy may contest you for the victory and you may have to come against him again and again until you drive him out.

Step Six: Jesus Christ has given you the power of binding and loosing. Use your authority in Jesus Christ along with the principle of two or more agreeing.

Step Seven: Don't settle for a good defense. Go after the enemy and drive him out of your entire mind and personality until you are totally free.

HOW TO CONQUER DEPRESSION

Sometimes life can bring a vague sense of darkness, despair, and gloom. Many times there are specific reasons why we are depressed and other times it is a vague but strong feeling. Our thoughts—negative or positive—produce chemicals in our brain and body which actually intensify such feelings. There also can be spiritual forces behind depression which must be dealt with in order to experience release and freedom.

There are two ways to deal with depression and find release, freedom, joy, and peace. First, understand the source of the depression. There are perhaps very specific reasons we are depressed—marital difficulties, financial problems, or any other problem that can leave us feeling hopeless and discouraged. Second, there may be no apparent reason for our depression; we just feel dull, lifeless, and intensely gloomy. Sometimes depression can be a signal that we are in need of God's presence to solve problems we have been trying to solve on our own. The solution to all depression is to invite Jesus Christ and the light of His kingdom into our midst.

The key to release from depression is to employ *The Principle of Praise and Worship.* Once we begin praising and worshipping the Lord, our problems and depression have a way of fleeing like the morning dew on a summer day. First, by praising and worshipping God out loud, we cause the enemy to flee from our midst. The enemy cannot stand the praises of God's people. We break the spiritual forces of darkness when we worship the Lord.

Second, worship and praise to God invites the Holy Spirit and God's presence in our midst. It allows Jesus Christ to dwell among us and releases the light of His kingdom. Ultimately, depression is a form of spiritual darkness whether it is caused mentally, emotionally, spiritually, or biologically. Depression must flee in God's presence because God is light and in Him there is no darkness at all. God's glory is the magnificence of His presence in which healing, deliverance, and miracles take place. "But for you who fear My name the sun of righteousness will rise with healing in its wings; and you will go forth and skip about like calves from the stall" (Mal. 4:2).

The following is a prayer of worship and praise, suggested as a way to be released from depression. It is simply one kind of prayer; the Lord may lead you to pray an entirely different prayer.

Prayer for Release from Depression:

Father, I come to you in the name of Jesus Christ praising you and worshiping you! I praise you, God, and thank you for my life and the many good things that you have given me. I praise and worship you, Jesus, and thank you for my many blessings. I give glory to your name O God and worship you.

I praise your Holy Name, God! I worship you in Spirit and Truth. Father, I ask you to cleanse me of anything in my heart and life that displeases you. I ask that the blood of Jesus Christ cleanse me of all sins. If I have any root of bitterness or if I have given in to worry or have done anything in thought, word, or deed to displease you, I ask for your forgiveness right now, Jesus, and thank you for it.

Father, I come to you in the name of Jesus Christ and ask you to fill me afresh with your Holy Spirit. I praise you, God, for filling me to overflowing with a fresh outpouring of your Spirit. I also thank you for delivering me from depression and the spirit of fear. I praise your name. Thank you, God, for sending joy and peace to me in the name of Jesus. Glory to your name! I ask that your peace and presence would now surround me in Jesus' name, Amen.

47

CHRIST IN YOU

From the moment I invited Jesus in to forgive me of my sins, something happened to change my life forever. To begin with, on an intellectual level I did not understand what I was doing, because in my mind, I did not even believe in sin. However, Christ was faithful and literally came into my human spirit and brought me light. When I invited Christ into my life by faith, He actually came inside of me and began to live in me.

Sometimes we forget the enormous wonder and power of what happens when people invite Jesus Christ into their lives. God actually begins to live inside of them. By receiving what Christ died on the cross to give us, and by being washed in His blood, we are brought into spiritual oneness with God. The sin which separated us from God is removed and we are reunited with Him.

This places us in the same position Adam and Eve were before the fall. We are born again in spirit and made righteous in Christ. On an eternal level we are going to live with God forever in a place called heaven. But something else happens and our bodies, minds, and emotions enter into the process of redemption.

When we invite Christ into our lives, things become possible to us as human beings that were never possible before. When Christ comes into you, old things pass away and all things become new. You have the mind of Christ, and you are now connected to the unlimited resources of the kingdom of heaven.

God wants you to understand who you now are in Christ. You have been given tremendous power, wisdom, and ability that begin right here on earth. The problem is we don't understand or believe that, because most of us have so many other problems down here on earth. That's why God gives us the ability to praise and worship Him. When we do, our perspective begins to change. We no longer see things through our fear and sin-based consciousness. We see things through the mind or perspective of Christ.

After we become Christians, we are no longer citizens of this present world system, although we live and have specific purposes in it. We are now citizens of heaven and are supposed to conduct ourselves accordingly. On practical terms this means we can now face life's present challenges with supernatural power and insight.

With the renewing of our minds, we are free to cease living in a cycle of fear. Then revelation comes that we are overcomers in Christ. As overcomers we live life from a powerful new place or perspective. You should experience a profound transformation. Your life should become brand new. Colors should be more intense, relationships more vibrant, sunsets more brilliant, and your love stronger. The reason is that you have begun to understand what it means to have Christ in you.

The devil has been blasting you with his flaming missiles and bombarding you with adversity to deceive you so that you will not learn who you really are. Temptation, sickness, poverty, discouragement, strife, and depression have been ripping through your life because your enemy knows you are getting close to understanding who you really are in Christ.

Once you understand you are God's child and He is now your Father because of Christ, then you are no longer part of an earthly family, but God's family. You are an heir of God and a joint heir with Christ. You then come into the knowledge of who you are in Christ and have no more reason to fear anything you might encounter in life, ever again.

48

HOW GOD CAN COME TO YOUR EMOTIONAL RESCUE

It is a fact of life that emotions are very changeable. Many times we just don't feel happy, saved, or like doing anything. Marriages are ruined because people don't feel in love. But emotions are often fickle and deceiving and they are not the basis on which we can or should run our lives.

The Amplified version of James 1:21 says: "So get rid of all uncleanness and the rampant outgrowth of wickedness, and in a humble (gentle, modest) spirit receive and welcome the Word which implanted and rooted (in your hearts) contains the power to save your souls." The Word of God is able to move deeply into our thoughts, minds, and emotions to cleanse and heal us. Our emotions are often the product of our thoughts and our thoughts are often the manifestation of our unredeemed minds. The result is a kind of emotional chaos and slavery to our emotions which block us from the emotional freedom Christ gives us.

When the Apostle Paul says "Rejoice in the Lord always; again I will say, rejoice!" (Phil. 4:4), he is saying this as a commandment from the Lord. In whatever place or circumstance we find ourselves in life, we are to rejoice in the Lord. This does not mean we rejoice when something bad happens to someone or that there is no place for grief, mourning, and sadness. But in our daily lives we are to cultivate an inner attitude of rejoicing and being thankful to God because this process fills us with the Holy Spirit and brings emotional and spiritual freedom.

I remember when, as a student at the University of Missouri, I was regularly invited to attend a Bible study just off the campus where Christians gathered to pray, praise, and worship the Lord. I had barely accepted Christ and had come out of the sex, drugs, and rock and roll culture. Yet when we gathered to sing songs of praise to the Lord, a wonderful, healing sense of peace and tranquility would come over me. In all my years of Eastern mysticism, blissful states, and drugs, I had never experienced such total peace of mind. God's presence, released upon us through worship, permeated my entire being and would rest upon me, even as I slept. Pain, fear, worry, and anxiety which caused me to do drugs and drink alcohol disappeared in the healing presence of the Lord. I had been to psychotherapists and counselors, but never had I found such complete and lasting peace of mind and soul. It was the calming peace of a gently-flowing river.

Many times after leaving the sanctuary at The Church On The Way on Sunday morning, attending the Gideon

Principle Prayer Meeting with my wife, or going to the prayer chapel, the Holy Spirit's presence would minister a powerful sense of peace, healing, and joy that would settle over us and remain throughout the entire day. Sometimes we would volunteer to take care of the children after church, and the rich presence of the Lord would abide with us while we were there. When His presence is dwelling in our soul and overflowing in our personalities, the Lord also brings us inner healing and emotional tranquility.

That is why the Apostle Paul says, "And the peace of God, which surpasses all comprehension, shall guard your hearts and your minds in Christ Jesus" (Phil. 4:7).

God's peace and presence will protect you from the ravages of fear, anxiety, and attacks of the devil. You will be set free emotionally and experience a peace, joy, and deliverance that cannot be achieved through any human means.

49

HOW TO RELEASE THE POWER OF GOD IN YOUR LIFE

God does not want you to live in slavery, but men and society may conspire to put you in bondage and manipulate you for their own purposes. God created you to be free and happy. This is your right as a child of God. Because of the fall, generational curses, sin, and attacks of the devil, we experience all kinds of oppression. However, the Apostle Paul tells us, "You know of Jesus of Nazareth, how God anointed Him with the Holy Spirit and with power, and how He went about doing good, and healing all who were oppressed by the devil; for God was with Him" (Acts 10:38).

This means that Jesus Christ has the power to do good, heal, save, and deliver you right now. It means that God has the power to heal, save, and deliver people you pray for. In all life situations God has the power to help and desires to help you.

Therefore, even though we may be damaged due to the fall and other circumstances, today Jesus Christ is still going about healing all those who are oppressed by the devil. But in order to have Him step into our problems and help us, there are many things we must do. Here are some steps we must take for God to help us:

Step One: We must actively pray for God's help for Him to move into any situation. "...Truly, truly, I say to you, if you shall ask the Father for anything, He will give it to you in My name" (John 16:23).

Step Two: After we ask God to help us, we must believe He is going to do what we ask. "Therefore I say to you, all things for which you pray and ask, believe that you have received them, and they shall be granted you" (Mark 11:24).

Step Three: Do not limit God with unbelief and small requests. Believe God for the impossible. "Call to Me, and I will answer you, and I will tell you great and mighty things, which you do not know" (Jer. 33:3). Expect God to do amazing things in your life!

GOD CAN RE-INVENT YOUR LIFE

Okay, suppose you have made a wreck of your life. Perhaps you have had a bad upbringing, you are an adult child of an alcoholic, you are a former alcoholic or drug abuser, or just your basic basket case who accepted Jesus Christ. No matter what kind of disaster you were in the past, the Gospel of Jesus Christ promises you a brand new beginning. You are not stuck with your life. That doesn't mean that you may not have to work through things or that you are immune from everything you have done in the past. *However, God has the power to re-invent your life!*

I was raised a child of an alcoholic. There were mental problems and a generational curse built into me and I was literally programmed to self-destruct. Years after drugs, promiscuous sex, and chaos, I began to burn out like a meteor crashing to earth. Even after accepting Jesus Christ, I pursued a lot of empty and meaningless careers in the entertainment business that prevented me from becoming a father and having children with my wife. Kristina also had a lot of dead-end programs built into her being as well as the effects of her family's generational curse. These prevented her from wanting to be a mother and she also pursued empty goals as an actress. There's nothing wrong with careers in the entertainment business or any field, but when they become your final integration point and substitute for God's plan for your life, there is a problem. Adult children of alcoholics may not be drinkers, but they can easily become workaholics and use careers as their addiction.

God has a powerful promise to everyone whose life, marriage, mind, and relationships do not work. The prophet Joel says:

> Then I will make up to you for the years that the swarming locust has eaten, the creeping locust, the stripping locust, and the gnawing locust ... And you shall have plenty to eat and be satisfied, and praise the name of the Lord your God, who has dealt wondrously with you; then My people will never be put to shame (Joel 2:25-26).

God promises to re-invent our life and completely re-build it, even after the enemy may have devoured it. The world may say your situation is hopeless. Psychology may say you are doomed, and doctors may say you are going to die. But God specializes in the impossible. I understand this firsthand, as does my wife. God re-deemed us from the generational curse. We were pro-grammed through fear and negative examples not to want children. We were modeled after failing marriag-es.

Yet, God healed our marriage (which was on the verge of divorce) by teaching us how to love one anoth-er. Then miraculously, after fourteen years of marriage, we had our first child after one doctor told us an opera-tion was needed. The healing and regenerative power of God renewed our minds and bodies and we experi-enced God's blessing.

My mind, which was a maze of confusion and pain, was restored by the power of Christ. My self-image was restored by God's Word and fellowship with the Body of Christ. After years of New Age and occultic involve-ment, my inner man was vulnerable to activity in the in-visible realm. Yet I experienced not only inner transformation, but the power of Christ's blood to deliver me from my previous sins.

I have seen alcoholics delivered, homosexuals have their sexuality reoriented, victims of child abuse healed, marriages restored, careers rebuilt, bodies healed, and constant testimonies of God's creative power to rebuild broken lives. The good news of the Gospel is that God still moves in peoples' lives powerfully. Now, I understand that you don't see that on the evening news and it won't appear in *Time* or *Newsweek*. It will not be taught in school. Nevertheless, the real God who exists and still answers prayer is very busy healing and restoring lives!

50

THE POWER OF THE HOLY SPIRIT

There is no substitute for the power of the Holy Spirit in your life. There is no way to live as a full human being and be really alive without being filled with the Holy Spirit. You were designed by your Creator to be filled with the Holy Spirit just as a car is engineered to run on gasoline. Being filled with the Holy Spirit is not a theological extra or something that is a Christian thing to do. Being filled with the Holy Spirit is as essential to the function and wholeness of the human personality as food and breathing is to the physical body.

Man was designed as a trinity of mind, body, and spirit. In the inner part of every human being is a container called the soul which is built by God to receive His Spirit. Without the infilling of His Spirit, we find ourselves unable to deal adequately with the problems and challenges of living.

I am one of millions who can attest to this. My life— even my Christian life— simply did not work until I was filled with the Spirit of God. There was a distinct point in my life when I asked Jesus Christ to baptize me with the Holy Spirit.

This took place in the library of a ministry called the Lamb's Club on Times Square in New York City. Reverend Carl Valente asked me if I would like to get baptized in the Holy Spirit, and he laid hands on me there in the library. As I praised and worshipped God, Jesus Christ baptized me in the Holy Spirit. It was as if I were literally kneeling at the feet of Jesus Christ and weeping. As I knelt before Him, I realized that I was in the presence of the most pure being in the universe—God—and my only response was to worship and praise Him. In His presence I felt His love radiate through me and accept me totally. I felt waves of baptizing power flow through me. It was as if a torch from heaven lit my heart and it was set on fire. Though there have been many seasons since in my Christian life, my heart has never ceased to burn with the flames of the Holy Spirit.

After my baptism in the Holy Spirit, I began to sense God's closeness as never before. I experienced a fresh desire to read His Word and understand it, and I had a new sense of power over sin and the devil. The baptism energized me and illuminated my personality.

THE POWER OF GOD

We do not live in a calm and peaceful world. Every day's newspapers give accounts of wars or famines in distant lands, events which, even though they are happening far away, cause us to respond with sadness and concern. Closer to home, we all have to deal with family troubles, difficulties with people around us, and so on. And we cannot remain indifferent to the many ills that beset our society, from the harm caused by a shrinking economy to the spread of the AIDS epidemic and the rise in the crime rate. It is no wonder that many people feel overwhelmed.

But still the words of Jesus Christ ring true, "... you shall receive power when the Holy Spirit has come upon you; and you shall be My witnesses both in Jerusalem, and in all Judea and Samaria, and even to the remotest part of the earth" (Acts 1:8). Jesus Christ made available to us supernatural power that can push back the forces of chaos. He has also given us kingdom authority so that we can preach the Gospel and take dominion with the demonstration of His Spirit and power.

Jesus Christ said, "He who believes in Me, as the Scripture said, 'From his innermost being shall flow rivers of living water.' But this He spoke of the Spirit, whom those who believed in Him were to receive; for the Spirit was not yet given, because Jesus was not yet glorified" (John 7:38-39). This flowing of rivers of living water can only occur after our inner beings are immersed or baptized in the Holy Spirit.

Each of us is created to walk and live in a supernatural dimension. Only when we have been filled with God's Spirit can we be full and complete human beings. When people have been filled with the Spirit of God, there is a presence about them which radiates from within. Their eyes literally shine forth a heavenly light.

God's Holy Spirit is the power source of the human personality. Kingdom power, creativity, intelligence, miracles, gifts of the Holy Spirit, all flow from the Spirit of God to within a person. Praise and worship release these divine attributes.

51

HOW TO RELEASE THE POWER OF GOD IN YOUR LIFE - PART II

Everyone will face problems incapable of being solved by our own unaided efforts. The solutions to these problems can only be found by asking God for His help and intervention.

"Call to Me, and I will answer you, and I will tell (show!) you great and mighty things, which you do not know" (Jer. 33:3). No matter how dark the situation, we have the promise of an infinite, personal God we can call on to show us great and mighty things concerning the problem or situation.

This is an awesome fact about the love of God for each of us, Who will answer you powerfully when you call on Him!

This is a life-changing truth and reality that can transform any situation. You are not alone in the universe. So when facing a seemingly hopeless problem, remember that you have at your disposal a resource beyond yourself, and that is God.

Below are listed the five keys to facing any problem:

1. Talk to God about any problem or situation you are facing.
2. Believe that God cares about you and your situation.
3. Expect Him to answer you and give you wisdom.
4. Don't limit Him with small expectations. Expect great and mighty answers based upon His Word.
5. Praise Him and thank Him for answering before and after He does.

RIVERS OF LIVING WATER IN YOUR INNERMOST BEING

Becoming baptized in the Holy Spirit will change the very depths of your being. You will be a different person.

You will be connected on a deep level with the life force of God, and His Spirit will flow through you with power and force. It says in the Book of Revelation, "And he showed me a river of the water of life, clear as crystal, coming from the throne of God and of the Lamb" (Rev. 22:1). That river of the water of life is God himself in the Person of the Holy Spirit. When you receive Jesus Christ, His Spirit comes into you and when you are baptized in the Holy Spirit, the rivers of the water of life bubble forth like a gushing fountain from your innermost being to refresh you.

The dynamic of this baptism of the Holy Spirit is personal breakthrough in your life. Once the Holy Spirit is released in your inner being, He begins to enter each room of your personality and subconscious with your permission to recreate and rebuild you. A common term for this would be restoration.

God's glory through the Holy Spirit begins to create you as a completely new person in Christ. By yielding to the Spirit of Christ we become partners in God's creation of ourselves all over again in His original image. An eternal destiny is being worked in you at this very moment.

God's dream for your life is beyond any dream you could possibly imagine and no one or no power can stop it! Nothing can prevent you from becoming what He intends for you if you cooperate with Him. The day is coming when you are going to stand on the shores of eternity and view a light so fantastic, with colors so rich, it is humanly impossible now to conceive it. This present world with all its absurdity and tragedy will be long gone. You will be far more than you ever dared dream. A completely new existence awaits you in eternity. But you don't have to wait to get involved with it. The power of the Holy Spirit is the foretaste of what is to come. I encourage you to embark on the most fantastic adventure of your life by completely opening up to God and what He wants to do in and through you.

52

BEARING FRUIT OR RUNNING ON EMPTY

Famous rock and roll singer Jackson Browne's hit song "Running on Empty" characterized an entire generation that basically felt hollow inside, yet still "kept on trucking," or going through the outward motions of life.

It is possible to go through these outward motions—in life, marriage, and ministry—while completely missing genuine intimacy with God or people. Jesus Christ outlined this spiritual principle:

> I am the true vine, and My Father is the vine-dresser. Every branch in Me that does not bear fruit, He takes away; and every branch that bears fruit, He prunes it, that it may bear more fruit. You are already clean because of the word which I have spoken to you. Abide in Me, and I in you. As the branch cannot bear fruit of itself, unless it abides in the vine, so neither can you, unless you

abide in Me. I am the vine, you are the branches; he who abides in Me, and I in him, he bears much fruit; for apart from Me you can do nothing. If anyone does not abide in Me, he is thrown away as a branch, and dries up; and they gather them, and cast them into the fire, and they are burned. If you abide in Me, and My words abide in you, ask whatever you wish, and it shall be done for you. By this is my Father glorified, that you bear much fruit, and so prove to be My disciples. Just as the Father has loved Me, I have also loved you; abide in My love. If you keep My commandments, you will abide in My love; just as I have kept My Father's commandments and abide in His love. These things I have spoken to you, that My joy may be in you, and that your joy may be made full.

(John 15:1-11)

Here we see the principle of spiritual fruitfulness outlined by Jesus Christ. The key is for each of us as believers to abide in Him! Bearing spiritual fruit and being fruitful is directly related to how close we are living to God. Fruitful ministry and lives cannot happen where people have become dry and withered branches, cut off from the true vine. Even good things and right things can become dead works if they are not a product of the genuine flow of the Holy Spirit's work.

Have you seen the Fruit of the Loom commercial where actors dressed as grapes and apples jump up and down and act silly?

I talked to one of those actors by phone when I was in New York to promote a play. He was a funny guy and enjoyed his work and made a lot of jokes about the Fruit of the Loom commercial. In one sense, the fun he had acting like a bunch of grapes is how we should be hanging out with Jesus and having fun delighting in Him. This is what a real relationship is all about. Billy Graham once warned a young minister, "Don't make an agony out of your religion." Dr. Graham was warning him not to make his spiritual life something arduous and burdensome. Dr. David Yonggi Cho also spoke about having fun in your walk with Christ when he gave a talk at our church.

This principle holds true in all areas of life. True, sometimes relationships and our walk with God require work, struggle, and intensity. But there should also be long periods of delighting in God. This is joyous intimacy and the dance of life. Successful entrepreneurs and artists understand the relationship between fun and productivity.

Great athletes are the same way. Rigorous exercise and grueling endurance is actually a way to get high. When we delight ourselves in the Lord and abide in Him, it should be a joy and pleasure; if not, then somewhere in our depths something is out of sync.

When we truly abide in Jesus, we are having a blast. It is like surfing on some great cosmic wave. Beware of people who talk in strange terms of going "deeper with God," but look gaunt, pale, and as if they had seen a ghost. It may sound spiritual and religious, but it is a subtle trap. Super spirituality can be a maze the enemy tricks us into entering, always seeking and never finding, always feeling a vague sense of guilt and unworthiness. Remember you were saved by faith and not works. In the same way, you walk and abide with Jesus Christ by faith. The key is to enjoy walking with Jesus as you would with a friend.

53

HOW TO ACTIVATE THE POWER IN GOD'S PROMISES

Wherever you may be, there are promises in God's Word concerning your situation and circumstance. Principle Number One is *you are not alone in the universe!* You must study, read, and meditate on the Scriptures so that you can find out for yourself exactly what God's promises are for you. In Psalm 37, we see numerous promises which apply to all of life. Psalm 37:1-5 reads:

> Do not fret because of evil doers, Be not envious toward wrongdoers. For they will wither quickly like the grass, and fade like the green herb. Trust in the Lord and do good. Dwell in the land and cultivate faithfulness. Delight yourself in the Lord; and He will give you the desires of your heart. Commit your way to the Lord, trust also in Him, and He will do it.

This passage should burn into you like a laser beam and clear the cobwebs from your mind. The God of space and time is saying you don't have to worry because He is on your side in every situation and difficulty.

There is a secret truth here that many people do not understand. It states in the Bible that there is nothing wrong with planning and hard work. God rewards the person who plans and is diligent. But there are powerful, secret promises available to people who walk with God. In the above passages are four powerful promises:

Promise #1: Do not become upset by the success and prosperity of those who don't acknowledge or obey God. He is absolutely fair, there is the Day of Judgment, and God knows how to prosper those who love Him.

Promise #2: If you trust God and do what He tells you to do then you will succeed!

Promise #3: If you delight yourself in God, which means fall in love and celebrate life with Him as you would your beloved human spouse, then He will give you the desires of your heart!

Promise #4: If you trust to Him your plans, choices, and dreams, He will make them happen.

The bottom line is that if you trust God, powerful promises will be unleashed on your behalf.

Later on in Psalm 37:7-11 we read:

> Rest in the Lord and wait patiently for Him; do not fret because of him who prospers in his way, because of the man who carries out wicked schemes. Cease from anger, and forsake wrath; do not fret, it leads only to evildoing. For evildoers will be cut off, but those who wait for the Lord, they will inherit the land. Yet a little while and the wicked man will be no more; and you will look carefully for his place, and he will not be there. But the humble will inherit the land, and will delight themselves in abundant prosperity.

A political leader, military expert, musician, and wise man, King David is telling us principles to enable us to succeed in life. But, we are admonished to rest our entire psychological and spiritual being in the Lord. This means we are to allow the peace of God which surpasses any understanding to fill our personalities.

The Bible talks about real peace built on a relationship with a real God who intimately cares for each one of us. We can rest in confidence that He will protect, care, and provide for us.

We are also told not to worry, be upset, or become jealous of evil people who seem to prosper for a time. We should always keep this truth in mind. Anyone who has worked for any large corporation has seen occasions where selfish and evil people have appeared to prosper or get undeserved promotions. In every stratum of life we have all seen bad people appear to prosper. The natural tendency is to say to ourselves, "Look at so and so, he is selfish and does wrong, but he got ahead and I didn't." We need to watch our thoughts at times like these because such thoughts can lead us to evil doing— either by emulating such people or becoming so angry in our spirit that it blocks the power of God from working. God wants us to realize He is able to reward and take care of those who love Him. But, remember that we live in a fallen world and sometimes evil people will prosper temporarily. We must remember, too, that in addition to God's promises there is also the reality of spiritual warfare. There is a real conflict between unseen powers which have a vested interest in opposing you and trying to block your success.

Instead of stewing over the prosperity of evil people, we are to meditate on the promises of God's Word and ponder them over and over again to delight ourselves in Him. We do this by living in a place of praise and worship to Him. We praise God, thank Him, and worship Him in the midst of our present circumstances and trust Him to work on our behalf. We are to act like people who really know and believe He is going to help see us through.

This is why it says those who wait for the Lord, they will inherit the land. Do you recall the plots of the old western movies? The villains usually came to town and caused a peck of problems, but in the end the hero always stopped them. Well, Jesus Christ is our hero and He will stop the villains in our lives.

In the 1960s westerns, like *The Good ,The Bad And The Ugly*, you are never sure whether good or evil will win. This is exactly the mind set God wants you to avoid. We need to renew our minds with the Word of God which very clearly states that evil will be punished and good rewarded. We must not allow ourselves to be influenced by our culture's confusion regarding basic moral principles upon which the universe is founded.

In Psalm 37:11 it says, "But the humble will inherit the land, and will delight themselves with abundant prosperity." It is the people who are humble before God who will receive prosperity. This Scripture is not talking about being other people's doormats. It is talking about biblical humility where you bow before God in your heart and follow His ways—which means following the laws of love regarding your fellow man.

These truths work in the corporation, political arena, the football field, the motion picture industry, or the schoolyard. If we trust Him, God is on our side. "For the arms of the wicked will be broken, but the Lord sustains the righteous" (Psalm 37:17). God knows how to stop evil people cold in their tracks. We must move through life waiting for the Lord and keeping His way and He will exalt you to inherit the land. This is unknown to those who don't know God. We possess this secret that the evil people and those who mock God cannot comprehend, and it is that God will move powerfully on your behalf in all situations. We read in Psalm 37:39-40, "But the salvation of the righteous is from the Lord; He is their strength in time of trouble. And the Lord helps them, and delivers them; He delivers them from the wicked and saves them, because they take refuge in Him."

Nothing can stand in the way of God helping those who love Him. We are to rejoice in that fact. There is a real God at work on behalf of those people who call on His name. These are powerful truths. God's promises are reliable, no matter who you are, where you are, or where you make your living. The promises of God can release power into your life that will enable you to be an overcomer in any circumstance in life!

54

HOW TO REALIZE THE DREAM GOD
PLACED INSIDE OF YOU

You are here on earth for a purpose, and that purpose is not endless suffering, bitter frustration, or disappointment. True, there may be seasons of these things, but as a whole, God put you here to bless you so that you could be a blessing to others.

God has placed a dream in your heart about your life purpose and He has given you the key to unlock it. That key is believing and trusting Him.

DON'T LET THE DREAM DIE

Bad circumstances and negative people can come against you like an army. Don't let the dream God placed inside you die! In the Old Testament, God gave Joseph the dream that he would rule a nation. Yet there were times his situation was so bad that the dream appeared impossible. Joseph was betrayed, sold into slavery, tempted, and thrown into prison. It was there, in the middle of prison, that God gave him the interpretation of Pharaoh's dream which catapulted Joseph into a position of authority second only to Pharaoh's own.

Many times we forget that when we have faithfully committed our way to walking with God, that Jesus is Lord over all our circumstances. It is easy to trust Him when everything is going our way. Our faith is purified when, in the power of the Holy Spirit, we face all the problems in our lives and deal with them in powerfully effective ways.

It is easy to read the stories of biblical heroes and to believe that they have no relevance to us today. But the purpose of these historic accounts is to show us how God can rescue and deliver us right where we are.

Christianity and the Bible can easily become irrelevant to the real world in which we live. If Jesus Christ saves, then He has to do it where we live now. It is in this crucible where our faith becomes real and when our faith is tested.

Witnessing, evangelism, churchgoing—these ultimately become meaningless unless we see God's power moving in people's lives. The Apostle Paul said, "For the kingdom of God does not consist in words but in power." If we trust God through the storms of adversities and believe in the dream He has placed inside our hearts, then His power will give birth to that dream and no man can block it. In the final analysis, God will bring each of us to an acid test of our faith, but God will never fail us.

THE PRINCIPLE OF PRAISE AND WORSHIP

An overriding principle in breakthrough is to live our very lives in worship and praise to the Lord. When we live our lives in a continual attitude of worship, we will find that His kingdom glory descends, shattering the boundaries hell seeks to place upon us. Praise and worship release kingdom authority, and the very glory of God moves into every aspect and dimension of our lives.

In John 4:23-24, Jesus Christ said, "But an hour is coming, and now is, when the true worshipers shall worship the Father in spirit and truth; for such people the Father seeks to be His worshipers. God is spirit, and those who worship Him must worship in spirit and truth."

Worship involves our whole being, body, soul, and spirit, taking its proper place before the Lord of all creation. Our entire inner man or woman actually resonates with a supernatural glow when we worship God in spirit and truth. It is like a heavenly tune-up on the engine of our being and we cannot operate properly without regular tune-ups of this sort.

The Principle of Praise and Worship releases God's presence and creates a fullness in our lives. His presence brings peace, joy, abundance, healing, prosperity, wisdom, guidance, and maximum enjoyment of life. Maximum life can only be found by living—not hiding—ourselves from the presence of God. The key to living our lives in the presence of God is to live in praise and worship to Him.

If you wish to contact Paul McGuire regarding speaking engagements for your church, singles group, convention, etc.
-or-
If you wish to receive Paul McGuire's newsletter or order tapes and other materials.

Please write:

Paul McGuire
P.O. Box 803001
Santa Clarita, CA 91380-3001